TEDBooks

Payoff

The Hidden Logic That Shapes
Our Motivations

DAN ARIELY

ILLUSTRATIONS BY MATT R. TROWER

TED Books
Simon & Schuster
New York London Toronto Sydney New Delhi

Simon & Schuster, Inc.
1230 Avenue of the Americas
New York, NY 10020

Copyright © 2016 by Dan Ariely

Portions of this book have been adapted from *Predictably Irrational: The Hidden Forces That Shape Our Decisions* (New York: HarperCollins, 2009); *The Upside of Irrationality: The Unexpected Benefits of Defying Logic at Work and Home* (New York: HarperCollins, 2010); and Dan Ariely's October 2012 TED Talk, "What Makes Us Feel Good About Our Work?"

First TED Books hardcover edition November 2016

TED BOOKS and colophon are registered trademarks of TED Conferences, LLC

SIMON & SCHUSTER and colophon are registered trademarks of Simon & Schuster, Inc.

For information about special discounts for bulk purchases, please contact Simon & Schuster Special Sales at 1-866-506-1949 or business@simonandschuster.com.

For information on licensing the TED Talk that accompanies this book, or other content partnerships with TED, please contact TEDBooks@TED.com.

Jacket and interior design by MGMT. design
Interior illustrations by Matt R. Trower

Manufactured in the United States of America

10 9 8 7 6 5 4 3

Library of Congress Cataloging-in-Publication Data

ISBN 978-1-5011-2004-6

ISBN 978-1-5011-2005-3 (ebook)

To the wonderful people in my life who have moved me forward, backward, and sideways. I only wish I told you more clearly and frequently how much you mean to me.

CONTENTS

Payoff

From Tragedy to Meaning and Motivation

On the complexity of motivation, and a personal story

We are the CEOs of our own lives. We work hard to spur ourselves to get up and go to work and do what we must do day after day. We also try to encourage the people working for and with us, those who are buying from and doing business with us, and even those who regulate us. We do this in our personal lives, too: from a very young age, kids try to persuade their parents to do things for them ("Dad, I'm too scared to do this!" or "All the other kids are on Snapchat"), with varying degrees of success. As adults, we try to encourage our significant others to do things for us ("Sweetie, I had such a stressful day today, can you please put the kids to bed and do the dishes?"). We attempt to get our kids to clean up their rooms and do their homework. We try to induce our neighbors to trim their hedges or help out with a block party.

Whatever our official job descriptions, we are all part-time motivators. Given that motivation is so central to our lives, what do we really know about it? What do we truly understand about how it operates and about its role in our lives? The assumption about motivation is that it is driven by a positive, external reward. Do this, get that. But what if the story of motivation is in fact much more intricate, complex, and fascinating than we've assumed?

This book explores the jungle of motivation's true nature, as well as our blindness to its strangeness and complexity. Rather than seeing motivation as a simple, rat-seeking-reward equation, my hope is to shed some light on this beautiful, deeply human, and psychologically complex world. Motivation is a forest full of twisting trees, unexplored rivers, threatening insects, weird plants, and colorful birds. This forest has many elements that we think matter a lot, but in fact don't. Even more, it's full of unusual details that we either ignore completely or don't think matter, but that turn out to be particularly important.

What is motivation, exactly? According to Merriam-Webster's online dictionary, the word is "the act or process of giving someone a reason for doing something"; it's also "the condition of being eager to act or work." And so this book is about what moves us to feel enthusiastic about what we're doing. It is about why we feel driven to slog through tasks that may appear on the surface to be thankless. It's also about the dire need for managers to better understand the deeper nature of what makes employees feel engaged at work and what they can do to make everyone feel happier and more committed. It's about connecting more deeply to what we do, to the outcome of our efforts, to others, and to our relationships. But, ultimately, this book is about what we really want out of life before we die.[1]

The Motivation Equation

Motivation—in the sense of being positively engaged to complete a task—is a much thornier problem than it seems at third glance. To think about the complexity of motivation, imagine that you are trying to write down an equation that would capture all of motivation's fundamental elements. Maybe it would look something like this:

Motivation = Money + Achievement + Happiness + Purpose + A Sense of Progress + Retirement Security + Caring About Others + Your Legacy + Status + Number of Young Kids at Home[2] + Pride + E + P + X + [All kinds of other elements]

Of course, money is an important part of this equation, but this equation also includes a long list of factors such as achievement, happiness, purpose, a sense of progress, our relationships with our colleagues, and so on.

Think about your job for a few minutes. If you wrote this equation for yourself, how large would be the role that money plays in your motivation compared with the effect of Achievement, Happiness, Purpose, a Sense of Progress, Retirement Security, Caring About Others, Your Legacy, Status, etc.?

As you can see, the list is long, it has many elements, and we don't fully understand the types and range of incentives that motivate us, much less how these different types of incentives interact with one another or add up to one big thing called "Motivation" with a capital M. The motivation equation also includes elements that appear not to have much to do with joy. In fact, one of the most fascinating things about motivation is that it often drives us to achievements that are difficult, challenging, and even painful. For me, this aspect of motivation is particularly interesting and important. Because it was one of the most challenging experiences of my life that ultimately helped me see the deep and wonderfully complex root of motivation. Allow me to explain.

Called to a Tragedy

A few summers ago, I was having dinner with a few old friends when my cell phone rang. A woman I didn't know told me that she got my phone number from a mutual acquaintance. She asked me to stop by the local hospital as soon as I could. This woman had read about a trauma that affected me as a teenager and thought I'd be able to offer some helpful advice to her best friend, someone I'll call "Alice." I deeply dislike hospitals for reasons that will soon become clear, but my motivation to help was stronger than my aversion. I couldn't refuse the request. I left my friends and headed to the hospital.

When I met Alice there, I learned that she and her family had just suffered a terrible tragedy: two of her teenage children had been badly burned in a fire. After describing their condition to me to the best of her ability, the distraught mother asked me what I thought she should tell her kids about their injuries. They were drifting between consciousness and unconsciousness, suffering awful pain and fear. Alice wanted to understand what they would want to know about their injuries, about the treatments ahead, and about their roads to recovery. She also asked me what they would not want to know.

She asked me about these things because she had heard of my personal story. Many years earlier, when I was a teenager, about 70 percent of my body was burned as the result of an accident. I spent about three years in a hospital. During that time, I underwent many treatments and surgeries. And I had been in a very similar situation to that of Alice's kids.

I did not know how to answer her questions, but I did my best to transport myself back in time to my own early days in the hospital. I remembered the noises. The hums and beeps of the machines. The equipment. The pain. The sounds of my fears. The phrase "pain person" echoed in my mind. It was a phrase that I must have heard at some point from the medical staff, and I took it to mean that I was someone who was completely engulfed in the intensity of the pain. Everything was defined by pain, and there was nothing else. No past and no future. There was only the pain of the moment. Nothing else.

One memory that came rushing at me from those early days in the hospital was the daily removal of my bandages. Because I had no skin, the bandages adhered to my raw flesh. The nurses would rip off the bandages, then rub the freshly wounded flesh to remove the dead tissue until they saw bleeding—a sign that the underlying tissue was alive. They would then put ointment on the wounds and rebandage my body. The next day, they would repeat this agonizing process. The only time I had a reprieve from the torture was on the days I had surgery, and sometimes the day after. Oh, how I looked forward to surgery, the bliss of anesthesia, and the few days of recovery.

I did not share my memories of the bandage removal with Alice, but I did tell her that when I was in the hospital, I wanted to know the meaning of all the noises and beeps around me. I wanted to know my heart rate and blood pressure. I wanted to know the level of oxygen in my blood, the functioning of my lungs, and so on. I wanted to know which sounds meant that my body was functioning and which indicated that things were not going well. I also wanted to know how long the pain would continue, when a treatment would cause the pain to increase, and when I would have some relief. At the superficial level, it seemed that I yearned for information about what was happening to me, but what I really wanted—in contrast to my almost motionless experience in the hospital bed—was to have some feeling of control. I described all of these things to Alice before I left.

A few days later, Alice called me, weeping. She asked me to return to the hospital. When I arrived, she told me that one of her kids had just passed away. She asked me whether she should tell her surviving son (I'll call him "Bill") about his brother's death. I had no idea what to say, but again I tried to transport myself back in time. I tried to think about how—in that world of pain and difficulty, of breathing and falling in and out of consciousness, of machines and being intubated, of hallucinations and painkillers—I might have dealt with news of such magnitude. I couldn't comprehend how anyone could handle the grief of losing a sibling on top of such pain and confusion, so I suggested that she keep the news from him as long as possible.

A few months later, I got some better news. Bill was out of immediate danger, fully conscious, and more or less aware of his situation. She asked me to send her son an optimistic note about his recovery and his future. Her request overwhelmed me with sadness. I knew all too well that this kid was just beginning to heal and that the road ahead would be long and brutal. It was going to be much harder than any of them imagined.

What could possibly motivate me to revisit the suffering I'd endured? As I reflected on Alice's request, I remembered the first time I walked out of my hospital room by myself. I got out of bed and shuffled to the door, opened it, and stepped out, proceeding very, very slowly and painfully. I was determined to make it all the way to the nurse's station. When I got there, I saw a big mirror. Without thinking, I took another step and looked at myself. It was hard to believe that the creature in the mirror was seventeen-year-old me.

Up to that point, I had seen different sections of my body from time to time, but this was the first time I had a full view. I saw legs that were deeply bent and covered with bandages and arms that appeared to be dangling lifelessly from my shoulders. My back was hunched over, and my face was a rainbow of colors.

The right side was completely blue and red and yellow. Pus oozed from different places; pieces of skin hung from my face. My right eye was swollen shut. Only the left eye, stuck in this strange disguise, seemed recognizable. The rest was very, very different than the healthy person I once was. It didn't look like an injured "me," because there was almost no resemblance to how I remembered myself; it looked like someone else. Only it wasn't.

After staring at the thing in the mirror for a few more moments, I couldn't stand the pain in my legs anymore. I turned around and shuffled as fast as I could back to the bed, where I struggled with pain for the next few hours. This time pain was my rescue. Unable to think about anything else, I returned to being a pain person.

I also remembered how, about a year and a half later, my scars were almost completely closed and I was in a much, much better state. But the improvements and the increased hope that came with feeling healthier were also accompanied by new and unexpected challenges. My scars—now red, thick, and slightly raised—had somehow developed the ability to shrink very quickly. Every time I would sit with my arms or legs bent for an hour or two, maybe watching TV or just resting, I wouldn't be able to straighten my limbs and neck because the scars would shrink just a little bit, limiting my range of movement. To get the scars to stretch back to their previous length, I would have to push and push against them, trying to straighten my arms and legs while almost tearing my skin. Sometimes I couldn't completely regain my range of movement. When this happened, I'd have to undergo a new operation to remove some of the tightened skin and replace it with new skin, only to go through the whole process again. I hated fighting my body all the time. It was betraying me, and I loathed the daily, never-ending, fight.

Torturous as the memories were, they also drove me to try to help Alice and Bill. Alice wanted me to send Bill a hopeful, positive note but, knowing what I knew, I asked myself: How optimistic should I be? What could I tell him? How honest could and should I be? The reality was that he was probably going to have a deeply miserable life for a very long time. I thought about all the treatments that I still had to undergo thirty years after the accident. It was not clear to me whether he was better off alive or dead (thoughts that I had had for years about my own painful existence). And it was not clear to me that his prolonged agony (another thought that I had had about myself) was better for him or his family.

Over the next forty-eight hours, as I relived my own experiences and struggled with what to say to Bill, I cried a lot. I wept more than I had in years. Finally, I came up with an outline for a message with which I was comfortable. Because I can't use my hands very well, I recorded a voice message to him and emailed it to Alice. I started by telling Bill that his life was going to be tough and that progress would be slow, but there was a way to live with his injury. I told him that technology helps everyone, but that it helps people with disabilities even more. I also told him that the modern workplace makes it possible to work and function in new and flexible ways that fit people with our kinds of challenges. I said, "For example, I chose the life of a university professor because it creates tremendous flexibility in my life. I can work more when I feel better and less when I am in pain. On top of that, while I can't use my hands very well, I can use voice technology to help me write my books and papers, and this technology is only getting better."

The whole process of creating my message for Bill was tremendously distressing, and I felt a great relief the moment I pressed the "send" button. Alice replied two days later, telling me how much my note had helped her son and how much she appreciated it. She asked me to send him another one, and—despite the difficulty of the first one—I have been sending him messages ever since.

A few months later, I went to see Bill in the hospital. I didn't get much sleep the night before because I was torn between my desires to help, on one hand, and my deep worry about how I would react to seeing him. (I had been back to hospitals quite a few times, but only as a patient, not as a visitor.) To my surprise, the visit with Bill was quite good. We talked about all kinds of topics—the hospital, life outside its walls, family, and the complexity of living with injuries and treatments.

After a few hours, a nurse came in and told Bill that he was going to have a new type of treatment, one that I remembered having myself. It was clear to everyone in the room that this new treatment would be painful. "Can we put it off a little bit, maybe until tomorrow?" he asked plaintively.

"I'm sorry, Bill, no. It has to be right now."

"Can't we just wait an hour or so?"

The nurse shook her head.

"Do we have to do it all over? Can't we just do one part of my body?"

"No, I'm sorry, sweetie."

At that point, I couldn't take it anymore. I became so anxious that I was unable to stand. I sat down, placed my hands on my knees, and put my head down, trying to breathe slowly. I remembered all the times I tried to negotiate with the nurses myself—trying to delay the treatment, reduce the pain, asking for only certain parts of my body to be treated on that day. Like Bill, I failed almost every time. The nurses' concession was not an option.

As I walked away from the hospital, trying to contain my emotions, I realized something new about my injury and the way it changed my life. Up to that point, when I thought about my own suffering, I had just focused on the pain. I thought about shrinking scars. I wondered what I looked like to other people. I thought about the difficulty of being unable to regulate my body's temperature, and the limitations of my movements—all the physical aspects of the injury. But observing Bill's failed negotiation, I realized the devastating role that helplessness played in my own experience. It made me more deeply appreciate the challenges of being badly injured, the complexity of recovery, and the ways that my experience had deeply changed me. I also realized how many of our motivations spring from trying to conquer a sense of helplessness and reclaim even a tiny modicum of control over our lives.

Pain and Meaning

What does my story have to do with human motivation? It shows how deeply we are driven to tap into a sense of meaning, even when doing so is challenging and painful. It also shows that there is a big difference between happiness and meaning. You might think that you would be happy to spend all your time sitting on a beautiful beach drinking mojitos (feel free to replace with a different activity of your choice). And that as long as you get to fill your days this way, you would be happy forever. But while a few days of hedonic bliss might be fun from time to time, I can't imagine that you would be fulfilled by spending your days, weeks, months, years, and life this way.

While perhaps unintuitive, research that examines the differences between meaning and happiness finds that the things that give us a sense of meaning don't necessarily make us happy. Moreover, people who report having meaningful lives are often more interested in doing things for others, while those who focus mostly on doing things for themselves report being only superficially happy.[3] Of course, "meaning" is a slippery concept, but its essential quality has to do with having a sense of purpose, value, and impact—of being involved in something bigger than the self.

The German philosopher Friedrich Nietzsche argued that life's greatest rewards spring from our experience of adversity. In my case, the stinging smell of the oily unguents, hearing Bill's screams and moans, seeing the empathic agony of his family brought me back to my own miserable experiences. It was all pretty terrible. But eventually, through my conversations with

Bill and his family, I achieved a complex but unique emotional lift that stemmed from shared pain. I became motivated by a feeling of identification and empathy for them. I felt that my own suffering had not been pointless. And that I could do something to help other human beings—something that I'm uniquely qualified to do.

We all know people who garner a great sense of meaning even in the most unpleasant of circumstances. A friend of mine who works as a hospice volunteer, for example, has spent years in companionship with people as they go through their last steps in life. She sits through long nights at their bedsides, holding their hands and singing softly to them. She sees herself as the "midwife of death." "It's the other end of birth," she says, "and I feel lucky to help them go through that door." Other volunteers clean smelly, sticky stuff off oil-soaked birds following a spill. Many people spend portions of their lives working in dangerous, war-torn areas, trying to keep disease and death from innocent civilians or teaching orphans to read. Their pain is real; their sense of doing something truly meaningful is substantial. They demonstrate how our ingrained desire to believe that our lives have purpose beyond our life span drives us to work extra hard, even to the point of our own personal suffering, in order to gain more meaning.

Even my nurses—adhering to their higher calling of healing me—clearly didn't enjoy ripping those bandages off while I screamed and begged them to stop. As awful as the experience was, it is also clear that they weren't trying to hurt me; they were doing their jobs as compassionate people working hard to make my life better. It certainly would have been much easier for them to delay the treatments a bit, leave the most painful parts for another day, and accept my deep gratitude for putting off the pain. But they didn't. They carried on with their difficult job despite its horrors and, over the years, brought me to a much better place.

The point is that these seemingly odd and irrational motivations get us to do things that are complex, difficult, and unpleasant. But they go beyond helping people in need. They motivate us in every aspect of our lives—whether in our personal relationships, in our individual pursuits, or in the workplace. This is because human motivation is actually based on a time scale that is long, sometimes even longer than our lifetimes. We're motivated by meaning and connection because their effects extend beyond ourselves, beyond our social circle, and maybe even beyond our existence. We care deeply about meaning, we care about it more as we become aware of our own mortality—and if we have to go to hell and back in a search for meaning and connection, we will, and we will get deep satisfaction along the way.

In the end, human motivation is not simple, but as we understand it more, we'll better be able to handle ourselves, our work, our relationships, our employers, and our employees. Knowing what drives us and others is an essential step toward enhancing the inherent joy—and minimizing the confusion—in our lives.

1 How to Destroy Motivation, or: Work as a Prison Movie

Why it's astonishingly easy to demotivate someone

Life is never made unbearable by circumstances, but only by lack of meaning and purpose.

—Viktor E. Frankl

A few years ago, I was invited to speak about the topic of decision making to a group of a few hundred engineers at a big Seattle-based software firm. During the years before I met them, the mandate for this carefully recruited, experienced, and brainy bunch had been to create something fabulously innovative that would become the next big thing for this staid software company.

The engineers dove into the challenge with enthusiasm. They conducted tons of research. They built an almost-working prototype. They were all proud of their work, having spent long hours—including evenings and weekends away from their families—to make this awesome thing happen. They believed their invention would transform their company and make it the innovation giant it should have been.

After a short introduction, I started talking about some research that I was working on. I began by describing a set of experiments that Emir Kamenica (a professor at the University of Chicago), Drazen Prelec (a professor at MIT), and I had carried out—studies that unexpectedly resonated with the engineers.[4]

In these experiments, we asked participants to build some Lego Bionicles. These are marvelously weird Lego creatures that kids can creatively assemble in many different ways. We picked Bionicles as the object of our investigation because the joy of Lego is almost universal across cultures and ages, and because building with them resembles, at least conceptually, the creative process that is so central to innovation in the workplace.

We divided the participants into two different conditions. We offered the participants in one group $2 for the first Bionicle they built. We told them that at the end of the experiment, we would disassemble the Bionicles, put the pieces back in the box, and use the same Bionicle parts for the next participant. The participants seemed perfectly happy with this process.

After these participants assembled their first Bionicle, we placed their completed creations under the table for later disassembly. We then asked: "Would you like to build another one, this time for eleven cents less, for $1.89?" If the person said yes, we gave him another one, and when they finished that one, we asked, "Do you want to build another?" this time for $1.78, another for $1.67, and so on. At some point, the participants said, "No more. It's not worth it for me." On average, participants in this condition built eleven Bionicles for a total take-home pay of a bit more than $14.

The participants in the second condition were promised the same amount of money per Bionicle, so they had the same financial incentive. But this time, as soon as they finished building a Bionicle and started working on the next one, we began disassembling their completed Bionicle. Right before their eyes. Once we finished undoing their work, we placed the parts back in the box.

The first group built their Bionicles in what we called the "meaningful" condition, so called because they were allowed to feel that they had completed their work satisfactorily. We called the second condition the "Sisyphic" condition—named after the ancient Greek story about Sisyphus, who was condemned by the gods to roll a boulder up a hill only to have it roll down again and again for eternity. Those in the Sisyphic condition managed to build an average of seven Bionicles—four fewer than those in the "meaningful" condition.

As I described this experiment to the engineers, I added that we also looked at individual differences in terms of Lego love. Some people are naturally enthusiastic about building Bionicles, while others not so much. We wanted to see how this individual difference translated to productivity. In the meaningful condition, some participants were unenthusiastic about making Bionicles, so they made fewer of them. In contrast, those who loved making these creations were happy to assemble them for relatively small amounts of money. Basically, people who loved the task kept on going because they enjoyed the process and found meaning in it. (Of course, we weren't talking about Meaning with a capital *M*. These folks weren't curing cancer or building bridges; they were building plastic toys, and they understood that their creatures would be taken apart quite soon.)

But here's what was so interesting: In the Sisyphic condition, we discovered that there was no relationship between the internal joy of making Bionicles and productivity. Those who weren't terribly excited about Bionicles created about seven of them—the same number as those who loved building them. In general, we should expect that those who love Bionicles would build more of them, but by dismantling their creations right before their eyes, we crushed any joy that the Bionicle-loving participants could get out of this otherwise fun activity.

As I was describing these results, one of the chief engineers stopped me. "We completely understand the experiment you're talking about," he said, "because we've all just been part of the Sisyphic condition."

They all nodded in sorrowful agreement. The chief engineer continued talking. "Last week, our CEO told us that our project was canceled, that the whole initiative was going to be scrapped, and that soon we would be assigned to other projects."

Up to that point, I had wondered why the people sitting in front of me were so lethargic and depressed. Now I understood.

"Your situation," I told them, "is also the way that some movies depict breaking the spirit of prisoners. Does anyone here remember the famous prison-yard scene from the movie *The Last Castle*?"

Several people nodded. In the movie, Robert Redford plays the role of Eugene Irwin, a court-martialed three-star lieutenant general who is sentenced to ten years in prison. Soon

MEANINGLESS
WORK FEELS LIKE:

MEANINGFUL
WORK FEELS LIKE:

after he is imprisoned, he challenges the warden over the bad treatment of prisoners and is punished for insubordination. His punishment is to move enormous rocks from one side of the prison yard to another. The task is so daunting that many of the prisoners think he will pass out before finishing; others cheer him on. After hours of back-breaking work, Irwin manages a final push of energy. He pulls up the last huge rock, carries it across the yard, and drops it triumphantly onto the pile. The prisoners go wild. It looks like a happy ending—until a few seconds later when the warden tells the prisoner he's not finished with the job and orders him to put the rocks back.

Irwin continues to move the rocks back until sunset, but, though he accomplishes this harsh punishment, there is no sign of triumph from him or his fellow prisoners.

"What added to the torture," I explained to the engineers, "wasn't just that he had to carry all those terribly heavy rocks; it was the fact that the goal of moving them from one side of the prison yard to the other was taken away. And by forcing Irwin to put the rocks back, the warden drained him and all the prisoners of any potential feeling of accomplishment, making the victory a hollow one. This type of futile battle is the same as Sisyphus's." I added, "If Sisyphus were pushing his rock up a new hill every time, he would have a sense of progress. But because he keeps pushing the same rock up the same hill over and over, his work is completely meaningless."

That's when I overheard one of the engineers sitting in the front row mumble to another, "So we're basically working in a prison movie."

Shredding Motivation

The connection between our experiments and how events unfolded in the lives of the software engineers was uncanny. I immediately felt both connected to them and sorry for them, as their work had been brutally robbed of meaning. I am not sure whether, at that point in the conversation, I should have moved to a less charged topic, but I was so fascinated by the unexpected match between our Bionicle experiments and the engineers' experience that I decided to push forward and describe a few more experiments on motivation and futility at work.

"In another experiment, we printed letters in random order on many sheets of paper," I explained. "We then asked participants to find pairs of identical letters that were next to each other."

When participants finished the first sheet, they were paid 55 cents. We then asked them if they wanted to do another sheet for 5 cents less, and so on. (This was the same diminishing-payment approach we used in the Bionicles experiment, just with a different task and different amounts of money.) In this experiment, we had three conditions. In the "acknowledged" condition, each participant wrote their name on the top left of the sheet, found all the pairs of letters they could, and then walked over to the experimenter and gave the paper to him. The experimenter looked at it carefully from top to bottom, said "Uh-huh," and placed it facedown on a pile on the left side of his desk. He then asked the participant if he or she wanted to work on another sheet for five cents less, or if

they would rather stop and get paid for their work. If the participant wanted another sheet, the process continued.

The "ignored" condition was slightly less meaningful. This
time, the participants didn't write their names down, and when
they handed in their sheets, the experimenter didn't even look
at their papers. He simply placed them facedown in a pile on the
left side of his desk without any kind of acknowledgment.

We called the last and most extreme condition the "shredded" condition. In this condition, when participants handed
their sheets to the experimenter, they were not acknowledged
at all. The experimenter just inserted the sheets into a large
shredder next to his desk. He then turned to the participants
and asked if they wanted to do another sheet for a payment of 5
cents less.

You might reason that those in the "ignored" condition
would have quickly learned once they completed their first sheet
that they could cheat. No one was checking their work, so why
bother finding all the pairs of letters? Why not earn more money
for less work? You could also reason that the temptation to cheat
would be even stronger for those in the "shredded" condition.
Why not shirk and get paid for doing nothing? If this were the
case, we thought we would find that participants in the "ignored" and "shredded" conditions would have chosen to work
longer for less money. But did they?

Here is what we found: In the "acknowledged" condition, participants stopped when the pay rate fell to around 15
cents—indicating that doing more was not worth their time.

In contrast, participants in the "shredded" condition stopped working far earlier, at about 29 cents. These results show that when we are acknowledged for our work, we are willing to work harder for less pay, and when we are not acknowledged, we lose much of our motivation.

What about the "ignored" condition? You might think it would be somewhere between the "acknowledged" and the "shredded" conditions, but where? Would the results fall closer to the "acknowledged" or to those of the "shredded" condition? Perhaps exactly in the middle?

In fact, participants who experienced the "ignored" condition stopped working when the payment per page was around 27.5 cents—only 1.5 cents less than the participants whose work was shredded. This suggests that if you really want to demotivate people, "shredding" their work is the way to go, but that you can get almost all the way there simply by ignoring their efforts. Acknowledgment is a kind of human magic—a small human connection, a gift from one person to another that translates into a much larger, more meaningful outcome. On the positive side, these results also show that we can increase motivation simply by acknowledging the efforts of those working with us.

As I described these results and their implications, the software engineers looked increasingly grumpy. Sadly, there are many employees of many companies in the same state.

According to Gallup, which has been collecting data on employee engagement for many years, American workers are generally unmotivated in their jobs—a problem that has risen steadily by about 2 percent a year since Gallup began examining this issue in 2000. Today, more than 50 percent of employees are disengaged, while only about 17 percent are "actively disengaged."[5] Negative motivation is a big deal, because when people are disengaged, they show up late, they leave early, they fail to keep on top of their expense accounts, they do the least that they can, and sometimes they even actively sabotage their employers.

Why are people so demotivated at work? I think it's partially because of the persistence of an industrial-era view of labor that is largely accepted as truth. This view holds that the labor market is a place where individuals exchange work for wages (regardless of how meaningless the labor is) and that people typically don't really care what happens to their work as long as they are fairly compensated for it.

This view of labor as a work-wage exchange springs from Adam Smith's 1776 magnum opus *The Wealth of Nations*, in which Smith described the benefits of breaking a large task into components, assigning one person to each specific task, and encouraging them to specialize in performing it. In his famous example of the pin factory, Smith argued that having one person make every part of a pin would result in low productivity. In contrast, he envisioned an efficient workplace built on a division of labor. It looked like this: "One man draws out the wire, another straights it, a third cuts it, a fourth points it, a fifth grinds it at the top for receiving a head."[6]

From the perspective of the factory owner in the Industrial Revolution, this approach of breaking tasks into components and letting people specialize in their specific tasks, bit by bit and hour after hour, yielded a lot of efficiency gains. But from the workers' point of view, this approach meant that they were nothing more than cogs in a wheel. They were working only to earn a wage, with no real sense of how their tasks fit into the big picture. From this industrial-era point of view, capitalism and labor were based on a simple equation: individuals needed and wanted stuff; companies made and shipped the stuff people wanted; laborers worked at dismal jobs for long hours so they could buy stuff. Workers were assumed to view work as unpleasant, but the reward was assumed to be so important (a paycheck) that it was worth suffering through to achieve it and then exchange it for stuff.

It's astonishing to me how some ideas endure even when it's obvious that they are no longer relevant. Smith's industrial-era view of labor has been passed down for generations as an indisputable truth, but as our experiments and many others show, there is a lot more to work than money and things to buy. As the great economist John Maynard Keynes observed, "If human nature felt no temptation to take a chance . . . no satisfaction (profit apart) in constructing a factory, a railway, a mine or a farm, there might not be much investment as a result of cold calculation . . . Enterprise only pretends to itself to be mainly motivated by the statement in its own prospectus."[7]

This is how I explained to the software engineers how their motivation equation got distorted. First, I asked them for their reflections.

"These days, how many of you show up to work later than you used to?" I asked.

Everybody raised their hands.

"How many of you now go home earlier than you used to?"

Again, they all raised their hands.

"How many of you now add not-so-kosher things to your expense reports?"

This time no one raised a hand, but later a few of them took me out to dinner and showed me how creative they could be with their expense accounts.

"Let's assume, for the moment," I continued, "that your CEO had to cancel the project for all kinds of legitimate reasons unbeknownst to you. What could he have done to make you less depressed about this outcome? Was there a way for him to cancel the project without demotivating you to this degree?"

"He could have asked us to build some next-generation prototypes and test how they would work," someone suggested.

"He could have asked us to think about which aspect of the technology we've been working on could fit with other projects in other parts of the organization," another engineer said.

"He could have asked us to make a presentation to the whole company about our journey over the last two years," another offered.

"All of these are reasonable suggestions," I said. "The problem is that each of these could require more expenditure of time, money, and effort, and it seems like your CEO doesn't see the value in investing more in this project simply because he doesn't understand the value of investing in your motivation."

That's when I told them about another fascinating experiment. This one didn't involve actual Bionicles or any physical tasks. It was a "prediction experiment" during which we ask people to forecast the outcome of a particular experiment.

Understanding predictions is important because we often face situations that force us to make decisions based on our intuition, without the ability to first test our hunches. For example, let's say you're a high school student thinking about going to college. You've read a lot about different schools and have even gone to visit two universities. You know a bit about each of them, but you don't really know how it would feel to study at either in terms of the quality of instruction, culture of the student body, and range of social activities. So you have to rely on your intuition, which may or may not correspond with reality. In fact, we have to use our intuition every time we don't have sufficient data, which is much of the time.

In the intuition experiment, we first described the procedures in the Sisyphic and the meaningful conditions to the participants—though we didn't explain the reasoning behind them. Then we asked them to imagine that they worked as consultants for a company that owned a Bionicle assembly facility. That facility used the "Sisyphic" method of production (identical to our experiment). We also told them that there was another assembly facility for sale—one that was not owned by their client. This other production facility used the "meaningful" method of production, in a way that was identical to our experiment.

We asked the "consultants" to predict by how much the number of assembled Bionicles would change if the client switched from their current "Sisyphic" assembly facility to the "meaningful" one. Would the number increase or decrease? And by how much? To answer this question, the participants had to intuit the motivation of the employees in both conditions and then predict the difference in the number of Bionicles created in the two production facilities. Basically, they had to predict the results of our original Bionicle experiment.

As it turned out, participants in this forecasting experiment thought that "employees" moving from a Sisyphic factory to a meaningful one would create only one more Bionicle. And as a consequence, they suggested that the CEO should pay just a tiny bit more to switch from the Sisyphic to the meaningful facility. In the real-life Bionicle experiment, production increased by about four Bionicles. In other words, when trying to intuit the outcome of these different conditions, participants predicted that the effect of meaning would be much smaller than it actually was. They greatly underestimated the power of meaning.

"This is important," I told the engineers, "because if your CEO is working according to his intuition and not data, and if his intuition is the same as that of the participants in our consultant experiment, this means that *he may be systematically underestimating the importance of meaning at work.*

"The consultant experiment," I continued, "showed that people dramatically underappreciate the extent and depth to which a feeling of accomplishment influences people. Your CEO most likely reasoned that people who work for him are like rats in a maze, only instead of working for food, you work for a salary. If he wants you to start working toward a different goal, he probably thinks that all he needs to do is to direct you down a new path, and you will quickly start working toward the new goal. He seems not to appreciate the effect that stopping your big project would have on your internal motivation."

The heads around the room nodded. The engineers felt that they had been working in an environment somewhere between our Bionicle experiment and Adam Smith's pin factory. It is true that these engineers' jobs were much more interesting and that they received higher wages than our experimental participants or Smith's pin makers, not to mention their social and health benefits and the ample free T-shirts emblazoned with the company's logo. But their creation was taken apart before their eyes; they never got to see the equivalent of their "pins" finally assembled.

For a moment, close your eyes and imagine that you are one of those software engineers. You're in your late thirties or early forties, maybe with a young family at home. You've worked very hard through high school and college to earn great grades in computer science. Maybe you even earned an advanced degree. When the company hires you, you're proud to have been selected because you know it has a reputation for hiring the cream of the crop. You buy a house in the Seattle area, a big investment that represents your commitment to stay at the firm for a while. You work hard every day, often during evenings and weekends, to meet your deadlines. You've built strong connections with your colleagues. You may even define your identity in relation to your workplace. As the end of the big, two-year project nears, you feel increasingly confident in the value of what you and your fellow engineers are creating.

And then the CEO makes his stupefying announcement. When that happens, you feel as if all that investment—what you've put into your work, your home, your education, and those collegial relationships—goes *pfffft*, like a deflated balloon. It's not just the feeling of wasted work that disturbs you. Nor is it even what one may see as the CEO's blindness. It's the sense that your own *life* matters less—that who you are has been belittled somehow. You haven't been working just for a paycheck or even a vision for the company: you've been working for yourself by building something that you cared about, and now all of this is gone. The CEO's announcement snatches away not only your sense of trust, meaning, accomplishment, connection, and pride, but also some of your longer-term dreams and hopes.

Given all of this, it's hardly surprising that some of the most innovative and senior engineers, now feeling "negatively motivated," quit the company a few weeks after my visit.

What Is Labor For?

The experiments I described to the engineers were all about actions that crush our natural motivation. Nobody can gain a deep sense of Meaning with a capital *M* from building Bionicles. Nor can anyone find a true sense of purpose from finding identical adjacent letters on sheets of paper. But the experiments told us a lot about how little it takes to kill even the tiniest enthusiasm.

There is also no question in my mind that the lessons from the software engineers, as well as the Bionicle and shredding experiments, apply to many work environments. With this in mind, we should systematically and carefully look for places where, by not thinking carefully about our incentives, we unintentionally damage motivation and productivity. For example, I know one very large company that takes its organizational hierarchy very seriously. They assign a number to each employee to reflect their level in the organizational hierarchy, and they use the organizational chart as the company's directory. This way, every time someone looks for a name, email, etc., they are reminded that they are at level X, that they are substitutable with other people at level X, that they are only a small part of a huge organization, that there are many layers above them in the company's hierarchy, and when they contact someone, their relative place in the hierarchy (and not their skill or contribution) dictates the tone of the discussion.

Another sad example that reduces motivation is the Dilbert-style identical cubicle that continuously reminds people that they are low in the hierarchy, not important enough to justify any investment in them, that the company is not expecting them to be around for a long time, and that they are basically replaceable. Cubicles are highly efficient, of course, from a space allocation perspective, but they don't add much to people's day. One company I know took the art of using cubicles to kill motivation to a higher level. They found out that employees had all kinds of personal mementoes on their desks, so the management redid the cubicles and made them 20 percent smaller, with less space for anything personal, but more space for more people. Another company came up with an even more brilliant idea that nobody could "own" their own cubicle, designing the system such that those who showed up to work earliest in the morning could claim the ones closest the windows. None of the cubicles has anything but a desk, a place to connect a computer, and a chair. No one could establish a sense of connection to their workspace. Ultimately, by setting the atmosphere this way, the company communicated to the employees that they are valued only for their direct productivity and that they are easily replaceable.

The good news is that we don't have to fall into these common motivation-killing traps. There are all kinds of things that companies can do to reinforce the feelings of meaning and connection in their employees. One important way to do this is to treat them as unique individuals not to be used, but rather to be appreciated and respected for their creativity and intelligence.

At the offices of Zappos, for example, employees are encouraged to be "weird." They decorate their cubicles in all kinds of wonderful, adventurous ways. Stuffed animals hang from ceilings; balloons are everywhere; the company looks like a cross between a party supply store and a toy shop, all in the service of fostering employees' sense of individuality and creativity. You might think that only little kids are motivated by this kind of environment. But the truth is that we never really grow up. A creative space, coupled with a kind word, genuine appreciation, the feeling of progress and achievement—the forces that motivate us are the same throughout our lives. In the adult world, companies are pseudo-parents, and they can be nurturing or quashing, enlightened or limiting.

By focusing on that which gives us a sense of meaning and connection, we will not only stop destroying motivation, but we can start growing more of this incredible resource. There is plenty of marvelous human energy lying dormant within most of us. And once those of us who are parents, teachers, and managers learn how to better tap into it, the better off we will all be.

HOW TO MOTIVATE YOURSELF

From time to time, we find ourselves bored and unmotivated at work or at home. Like Sisyphus, we end up doing the same humdrum, unrewarding thing over and over. What can we do to change the situation when it is impossible to change the circumstances? The answer: change your mental framing.

For example, a young man I know recently took a job at a hospital, disposing of waste and cleaning surgical equipment. After a few months on the job, he found it so boring that he considered quitting. But his mother reminded him that he had one of the most important jobs in the hospital because people in hospitals are especially vulnerable to killer germs like staph. Without his important work, she explained, these patients could easily become sicker and die. This shift in perspective renewed his pride in his job. He performed it with more energy, and not too long afterward he received a promotion. This example suggests that if we are feeling bored and unmotivated, we can ask ourselves: How is the work I'm doing helping someone down the road? What meaning can I find here? With this type of mind-set, chances are that we will be able to find a positive answer.

We can also try to find a creative or learning opportunity in our Sisyphic experience. I once asked a Broadway actor how he managed to perform the same play, night after night, month after month, and year after year without getting bored. (I was looking for tips, because I was getting bored with giving lectures.) The actor told me that he thought about doing something differently each time he performed. He experimented with different gestures, timing, and pauses, different emphases on words or passages, and different approaches to his character. He also took mental notes on how his little tweaks went over with the audience. In that way, the work became much more interesting. Borrowing from him, I now do the same thing. By gauging students' reactions to my little adjustments, I find that my routine work becomes much more interesting, both to them and to me.

2 The Joy of (Even Thinking That We Are) Making Something

On our deep attachment to our own ideas and creations

While reducing the harmful elements on motivation should be our first step, we also need to look closely at the positive side of motivation and think of ways to increase it. By understanding the building blocks of motivation, we can structure both our workplaces and our personal lives in ways that will make us more productive, more fulfilled, and happier.

But how can we increase motivation? To answer this question, let's think again about building something—this time, not a piece of software or a Bionicle, but a piece of IKEA furniture. IKEA came up with a brilliantly diabolical idea: the company would offer boxes of Bionicle-like furniture parts and make customers assemble the pieces by themselves, with only the help of their bitterly impossible-to-understand instructions.

I like the clean, simple design of IKEA furniture when I see it in their showrooms. But long ago, I found that assembling a piece of IKEA furniture—in my case, a chest of drawers for my kids' toys—demands a surprising amount of time and effort. I still remember how confused I was by the instructions that came with the chest. Some parts seemed to be missing. I put some pieces together the wrong way more than once. Overall, I can't say that I enjoyed the process. But when I finally finished building the piece, I experienced a somewhat odd and unexpected sense of satisfaction. I stood back looking at the chest and smiled with pride at having completed the job. Over the years, I've noticed that I look at that chest of drawers more often, and more fondly, than any other piece of furniture in my house.

My colleagues Mike Norton (a professor at Harvard University), Daniel Mochon (a professor at Tulane University), and I described the general over-fondness we have for stuff we've made ourselves as the "IKEA effect." And while IKEA inspired our original research, IKEA was hardly the first to understand the value of self-assembly.

Consider the history of cake mixes. Back in the 1940s, when most women worked at home, a company called P. Duff and Sons introduced boxed cake mixes. The mixes were almost ready-made; housewives had only to add water, stir up the mix in a bowl, pour the batter into a cake pan, bake it at 350 degrees for half an hour, and voilà! They had a tasty dessert to serve to their family and friends. But surprisingly, these mixes didn't sell well. The reason had nothing to do with the taste. It had to do with the complexity of the process—but not in the way we usually think about complexity.

Duff discovered that the '40s-era housewives felt that the just-add-water-cakes were a shade shy of buying ready-made from a store. Sure, the cakes emerged warm from the oven and the mix saved time, but the completed cakes did not feel like the housewives' own creations. There was simply too little effort involved to confer a sense of creation and meaningful ownership.

To solve this problem, the company took the eggs and milk powder out of the mix and put the new, harder-to-use mix on supermarket shelves. This time, when the housewives added fresh eggs, oil, and real milk, they felt like they'd participated in the making and were much happier with the end product. When someone told them, "What a delicious cake you made!" they could smile and respond: "It's an ancient family recipe." They didn't just accept the compliment; they believed they deserved it.[8]

The Duff cake mix story offers a simple and clear example of the power of effort and ownership and how it relates to motivation. It shows that when we work harder and spend a bit more time and effort, we feel a greater sense of ownership and thus enjoy more the fruits of our efforts.

My Beautiful Creature

To examine the "IKEA effect" in a more controlled, experimental way, Daniel, Mike, and I asked participants to work for us by making some origami creations in exchange for an hourly wage. We equipped them with colored paper and standard written origami instructions that showed where to crease the paper and the direction to fold it in order to create paper cranes and frogs, and off they went.

Now, folding a piece of paper into an elegant creation is harder than it looks. And since these participants were all origami novices, none of their creations was a terribly satisfying work of art.

When their temporary employment ended, we told them, "Look, this origami crane you just made really belongs to us because we paid you for your time. But we'll tell you what—we might be persuaded to sell it to you. Please write down the maximum amount of money that you would be willing to pay in order to take your origami creation home with you."

We called these people "builders," and we contrasted their enthusiasm for their origami creatures as measured by their willingness to pay for them with that of a more objective group we called "buyers." Buyers were people who had not made any origami; they simply evaluated the builders' creations and indicated how much they would be willing to pay for them. It turned out that the builders were willing to pay *five times more* for their handmade creations than the buyers were.[9]

Now, imagine that you are one of these origami builders imbued with such a deep affection and overvaluation for your work. Do you recognize that other people don't see your lovely creation in the same way that you do? Or do you mistakenly think that everyone shares your appreciation?

Before answering this question, consider toddlers. Little kids have an egocentric perspective; they believe that when they close their eyes and can't see other people, other people can't see them. As children grow older, they outgrow that kind of egocentric bias. But do we ever get rid of it completely? We don't!

We found that the egocentric bias is also alive and well in adults. Love for one's handiwork is indeed blind. Our builders not only overvalued their own creations, they also erroneously believed other people would love their origami art as much as they did.

But wait, there's more. In the "impossible" version of this experiment, we made the origami-folding task more complex by eliminating some of the most crucial details of the instructions. The standard set of instructions for origami includes arrows and arcs that tell the user what to fold and in which direction. The usual instructions also include a legend that tells the user how to interpret these arrows and arcs. In this more difficult version, we eliminated the legend, making the instructions useless and the whole process much harder. This time, our participants' creations were even uglier. As a consequence, buyers were willing to pay even less for the origami, but such objectivity was lost on the builders. In this "impossible" version, the builders valued their creations even more than when they had been given clear instructions, because they put extra effort into making them. Just as my working hard on the IKEA chest of drawers increased my affection for the damned thing, our origami experiments showed that the more effort people expend, the more they seem to care about their creations.

It is important to note that our experiments with Bionicles, paper shredding, and origami weren't connected in any way to one of the main drivers of motivation—our larger sense of identity. These tasks weren't life callings integral to participants' sense of themselves. Yet our participants' behavior clearly revealed that we are strongly motivated by identity, the need for recognition, a sense of accomplishment, and feeling of

creation. The finding that these needs played such large roles in our lab experiments suggests to me that the same thing happens in real-world work environments—but in spades. If, for example, you're a software engineer who has spent two years of your life working on a project, your identity is likely to be many times more powerfully connected to your creation than our participants' identities were to Bionicles or paper frogs.

Zappos, as we mentioned earlier, is a company that shows deep appreciation for the forces and complexity of motivation. As a place that wants very much to attract and keep talent, it focuses hard on employees as individuals and does everything it can to make people feel connected and happy. If someone is struggling with anything from weight loss to learning to write better, he or she can work with a coach. The facility in Las Vegas is designed to encourage connections and "collisions" so that as employees get up from their desks and walk around, they meet and exchange ideas. Employees are encouraged to do anything they can to wow customers; nobody takes customer service calls using a phone script. People are paid extra for learning new ideas and presenting what they learn to others. In hallways, you can find makeshift bowling alleys; employees wear costumes to work. One of Zappos's core values is "Create fun and a little weirdness." Zappos understands that we are all toddlers at heart, driven by play and a dash of individuality. All of these things make Zappos one of the "best companies to work for" according to *Fortune* magazine.

The Creating Consumer

It's easy to see how creators can garner a strong connection and a sense of identity and meaning from their accomplishments. It's also easy to see how this research applies to artists, crafts-people, and hobbyists. But what about the stuff we personalize as consumers? Henry Ford reportedly said, "Any customer can have a car painted any color that he wants so long as it is black." Those days are long gone. Now we can pick not only the color of our cars but the interior layout, the number of cup holders, the design of the wheel rims, and more. If you buy a pair of shoes online from Nike, you can customize the colors of the shoes, laces, and linings. A website called Chocomize lets you create your own special candy. M&M's lets you pick your color mix. At Zazzle, you can customize garments and cards to make them uniquely yours. Crowdfunding platforms now allow us to play roles in all kinds of creative projects, from art and fashion to film, games, technology, and more.

Initially, this desire to customize seems to be about preferences—we choose red over purple because we like red more. But the reality is that customization has additional bene-fits. By choosing red, we make the product a little more our own. And every time we choose a new color for our shoes, we person-alize them even more. The more effort we put into the design, the more likely we are to enjoy the end product.

So just think: 3-D printing is developing so quickly that one day, as consumers, we will soon not just design but also manu-facture all kinds of products, from picture frames to clothing to furniture and beyond. Regardless of what these objects might end up looking like, they will be much more meaningful to us than anything someone else has made because they will have the stamp of our own effort, design, care, and unique identity.

Home, Sweat Home

What kind of creation could be more customized and personal than a home? The intimacy and care with which we design our living spaces make home ownership an especially keen demonstration of the motivational power of creation. When I worked at MIT in Cambridge, Massachusetts, my wife, Sumi, and I owned a house close to the university. We loved the house and went to a great deal of inconvenience and expense to customize it. We renovated rooms, removed walls, and enlarged windows. After it was done (to the extent that renovations are ever done), we marveled at the open, airy feeling we'd created.

A few years later, when we moved to Duke University in Durham, North Carolina, we had to sell the Cambridge house. It sat on the market for a disturbingly long time. After several months, our real estate agent pointed out that most people didn't want to live with an open floor plan and recommended that we reinstall a few walls to make the space more closed and sectional. We were certain that she was wrong. Who would not appreciate the beauty of our open floor plan? Who would not love the feeling of warmth that comes from being able to see your children playing in the other areas of the house? So we resisted her suggestion for a while.

Eventually, we decided to follow her advice. And as soon as we added walls and closed up some rooms, a buyer snatched it up. The lesson: Just like the origami builders, Sumi and I too have an egocentric bias. Our taste is most likely just our taste, and very few people share it—but it was hard for us to truly appreciate and understand this.

Here's another fun ownership story from the annals of our Cambridge home-improvement efforts. Over the years, our renovations included many additional projects, including insulating the attic, installing a better heating system, renovating a bathroom, and, most excitingly, installing a sauna in the basement. The whole process involved all the typical delights that accompany such projects: broken promises, delays, unexpected surprises that ended up costing us more than the contractor's initial estimates, changes to the original plans that also ended up boosting the price, and so on. It was a long series of one annoyance after another (that we tried hard to frame as useful life lessons).

In general, the contractor didn't display much interest in installing plumbing, heating, or renovating the bathroom. One pleasant surprise, however, had to do with the construction of the new sauna. One evening, the contractor asked me to join him in the basement. "Look at this!" he said with immense pride. "We cut the wood for the walls and the benches this way." He showed me the fine grain of the wood cut, how the screws were elegantly bolted below the surface of the wood, the joining of the seams, and so on. I had to confess that although I had been irritated with him on many other levels, he created a wonderful sauna. In that project was evidence that he had a tremendous eye for detail.

His unusual level of artisan's pride made me wonder about the joy he felt in creating a completely new, standalone, and beautiful thing. It seemed that from his perspective, all the other aspects of the renovation were just fix-it jobs to be done and only incremental improvements. There was little that was creative or new about them. Moreover, any level of renovation was not even close to transforming the old thing into a perfect thing. The new windows sat in the old frames. The new heating system couldn't fit precisely in the old house. The renovated bathroom still maintained some of the old elements, including the uneven floor—which meant that the contractor could never feel that this was "his" bathroom. His creation. And without this feeling there was nothing in these everyday upgrades to encourage his best workmanship. But the contractor's gorgeous sauna was a complete *objet d'art* that he had taken a great deal of care to create from scratch. I suspect that for him, it stood as a tribute to his craftsmanship and creativity and was much more valuable in his own eyes than all the other work he had done.[10]

KIDS AND IDEAS

This attachment to one's own "custom" creation extends not only to physical things but also to ideas. This attachment begins surprisingly early. In an interesting set of experiments by Vivian Li, Alex Shaw, and Kristina Olson,[11] four-year-olds were presented with two identical sets of craft materials—five paper shapes and two cotton balls that could be glued together to make a design on a piece of construction paper. The experimenters told the children to think of an idea for a picture they could create using these materials and then to tell the experimenter exactly how to put all the pieces together.

Next, the children and the experimenter switched roles. The experimenter would think of an idea and tell the child where exactly to place the shapes. The children could pick their favorite picture and take it home. Which do you think that the kids preferred? The one that was the result of their idea or the one that was the result of their physical labor? If you, at your current age, were deciding, which one would you prefer?

By a pretty wide margin, the children picked the picture that was the outcome of their own idea, not the one where they provided the physical labor.

In another experiment, this time involving five-year-olds, researchers asked each child to dream up a story (for example, "Make up a story about a dragon and a little boy"). After the child invented the story, another adult entered the room, and the experimenter repeated the child's story by saying, "Tommy just told me the best story . . . !" In the "no-credit" condition, the experimenter told the other adult, "*I* have the best story . . . !" In this case, the children vociferously objected, saying, "That was *my* story!"[12]

What all of this means is that by a very young age, we already care about our ideas and are attached to them.

The Importance of Identity

Now, here is the question. If a simple task like making a Bionicle creature or circling letter pairs on a page can become more appealing by simply adding someone else's acknowledgment, and if people love their horrible origami creatures even more when they put more effort into them, how much more are we motivated to care about projects when we have truly invested all our heart, mind, and soul into them, as the Seattle engineers had done?

To think about this question, consider the greatest customization project of all—raising our own kids. Sumi and I are the parents of two incredibly adorable, intelligent, beautiful, and talented children (if we do say so ourselves) whom we love more than we ever imagined possible. Like all doting parents, we have spent endless sleepless nights and seen many a sunrise from the wrong side of the morning. We have changed our kids' diapers; succored them through sickness; dealt with their temper tantrums; splashed with them in rivers and oceans; put them to bed; fed them; driven them to school; helped them with homework; attended their soccer games, school performances, and countless birthday parties; placed Band-Aids on their skinned knees; and put money into their college funds. These labors of parenting are often challenging and sometimes unpleasant, but we are motivated to do them because of our enormous personal investment in our kids. When we look into their eyes and hear their laughter, we see purer and more adorable versions of ourselves. In short, we're heavily invested in our children in all kinds of ways—emotionally, financially, and with a deep sense of legacy that inherently extends beyond our life spans.

With this in mind, let's think for a few moments about kids within the context of the origami experiment. Say you are a parent who, like us, is highly invested in your own two incredibly adorable, intelligent, and talented children. For the sake of argument, let's say you find yourself in some kind of *The Twilight Zone*–style science fiction world where you take them to a park one day. In this parallel universe, another person plays with them for a few hours, is enchanted with them, and asks you, with all middle-class American earnestness, "Are your kids for sale?" She promises that they will have a good home and will be well cared for. What purchase price would you quote her?

In this alternate universe, most people would state a very, very high price (unless, of course, the kids in question are teenagers). But what if the situation were slightly different? What if you did not have any children, and you went to the park and met two wonderful kids who were very much like the ones you have in reality. You play with them for a few hours. As evening approaches and you get ready to say good-bye, the mother of the two children sidles up to you and says, "Wow! You have such a good connection with those kids! They are for sale. Are you interested?" How much would you offer her? (My guess is not much.)

This small thought experiment suggests that we think about our children as priceless, not just because we love them so much but because they are also *ours*. Raising kids is pretty much a DIY job. We put enormous amounts of effort into them, investing far more than a software engineer working for two years on a big project. The process is time-consuming and complex. Even if there were an instruction manual, it would doubtless be much less accurate than anything from IKEA, and even if it were clearly written, it would take a few lifetimes to read and understand.

The enormous effort we pour into our children also gives us meaning and connection, and it makes us think about them as the unique creatures they are. Certainly, it takes a lot of time and energy to play with them, help them with their homework, and the rest, just as it does to create a beautiful home or a beautiful piece of work; but the work itself rewards us, and we remember it with much affection later in our lives.

Thinking of our kids in this way can help us better understand the value that people place on their simple Bionicle creations or the value that Sumi and I projected onto our Cambridge house. We become more invested as we pour effort into different activities, and with it experience greater love for what we have created—our creations become part of ourselves and our identities. As an added bonus, we are all also largely blinded by our egocentric bias; we just don't seem to recognize that the love for the outcome of our own efforts is limited to us alone.

The same basic lessons of meaningful engagement, and our underappreciation for its role in our lives, also apply to many other aspects of our lives—which is why we often end up shying away from the more effortful and challenging experiences. If we have the money, we hire people to clean our houses, take care of our yards, or set up our wi-fi systems to avoid being bothered by these common annoyances. But think about the long-term joy we miss out on when we don't engage in such tasks. Could it be that when we trade off annoyance for more efficient task completion that we end up accomplishing more but at the cost of becoming more alienated from our work, the food we eat, our gardens, our homes, and even our social lives?

The lesson here is that a little sweat equity pays us back in meaning—and that is a high return.

3 Money Is from Mars, Pizza Is from Venus, and Compliments Are from Jupiter

Why money matters far less than we think

A man with glinting chestnut-brown hair stalks back and forth in a dingy office. A storm rages outside the windows. He eyes the men sitting before him with an aggressive indifference. He informs the team of humiliated real estate salesmen that they're in for a few hard weeks at the office, yelling in their faces like the world's most evil boot camp sergeant. He also tells them that there's a contest to see who can close the most sales. "The first prize is a Cadillac El Dorado," he tells them. "The second prize is a set of steak knives. The third prize? 'You're fired.'"

This infamous, insulting motivational speech delivered by a young Alec Baldwin in the movie *Glengarry Glen Ross* is an obscenity-studded caricature of the business world's cruelty. This scene—with its "ABC" ("Always Be Closing") directive—is often listed as a "must watch" for management trainees, reflecting the strong, persistent, and mistaken belief that external motivations, such as threats, are crucial ingredients in the recipe for inspiring hard work.

Movies aside, this type of cattle-prod threat is unlikely to fly in the modern workplace. But what about positive incentives such as annual and spot bonuses? Promotions? Titles? Company retreats? Health and retirement benefits? Which types of positive motivators inspire more dedicated work? Should management offer free coffee only to the employees who close deals? Should companies give more vacation time or better health benefits to those who achieve their quarterly goals? Should they assign nicer offices to the employees who more frequently stay at work after hours? All of these questions point to a broader one, which is, What kinds of external rewards are best at positively motivating people?

Because motivation is a part of almost everything we do, and because it influences and sustains virtually every aspect of our lives, it is impossible to come up with one simple set of motivational rules. We could consider the general question by imagining motivating the people of a war-ravaged nation, the United Nations, or an NBA team. The directives would be quite different for each group. Let's start small and imagine that you are the CEO of a tiny startup company. Until now, your company has had only one amazing employee (you). Now, you are ready to hire. Your next task is to set up the principles, rules, and regulations for how this company will treat future employees. There is no *Workplace for Dummies* book from which you can learn exactly how to structure your firm's approach to its workforce. Instead, you have to figure out the best way to train, manage, and retain your staff. You need to create the company's hierarchy from the person at the top down to the newest hire. You must set up a payment system: Will you pay people by the hour, by the job, by total output, by the number of days in which no one makes any mistakes? And what about health care benefits and bonuses? Daily? Weekly? Monthly? Yearly? What should your sick and vacation policies be? What is the right mix of intangible (praise, camaraderie) and tangible (salary, bonuses, gifts) benefits that will encourage people to give their best?

RATIONAL REGULATION

As if setting up the motivational forces at work is not sufficiently complex, consider the even more complex task of policymakers. When policymakers set up regulations, they are trying to create sets of motivations that, combined, compel us to behave the way they want us to behave.

For example, consider massive regulations such as the No Child Left Behind (now defunct) or the Affordable Care Act. These complex policies use a mix of incentives that range from financial rewards to penalties, from prohibitions and restrictions to public pride and shaming (also known as "accountability"). All of these positive and negative incentives are designed to spur specific intended behaviors and fix the problems in education and health care.

Of course, in practice, these policies have not repaired education or health care (and some argue that they have made things worse). I suspect that many of their shortcomings stem from a mistake on the part of policymakers: They did not start by examining the nuanced motivations of teachers and medical professionals. Most likely, they did not ask themselves: "Where do these professionals excel already? Where don't they need any additional motivation? Where do they struggle and need an extra boost? Which types of additional motivations would work best?" Instead of asking specific questions about motivation, policymakers most commonly conceive of policies as a big hammer and see teachers and medical professionals as a uniform set of nails. They apply the simple payment-for-performance, rat-in-a-maze understanding of work as an exchange of money and labor, which as we'll see, often misses the point.

An Experiment at Intel

Because the problem of determining the best way to motivate people is so vast and context dependent, there isn't (nor will there ever be) one experiment that would give us the one true answer to this question. Researchers can take only small steps in hopes of discovering how managers and policymakers can make slightly less damaging mistakes in their attempts to motivate people.

Quite a few years ago, Uri Gneezy (a professor at the University of San Diego California), George Loewenstein (a professor at Carnegie Mellon University), Nina Mazar (a professor at the University of Toronto), and I carried out some lab experiments on the effectiveness of large bonuses.[13] One of our main findings was that when the bonus size became very large, performance decreased dramatically. This counterintuitive effect stemmed from the stress and fear of possibly not getting the bonus. But that was a lab result. And since the laboratory environment is inherently limited in its ability to capture the true, complex nature of labor, we've spent years searching for ways to experiment with real employees at their workplaces. We wanted to study bonuses because almost all companies use some type of bonus, yet despite their ubiquity—and the fact that compensation is most businesses' *largest expense*—little is known about how effective bonuses really are. Even less is understood about what forms of payment work best. So understanding the effects of bonuses became our white whale.

When looking for a promising testing ground for experiments on motivation and performance, we thought about the types of jobs that would be best and worst to study. Defining the best jobs to study is complex, but we can probably agree that one of the worst types of job anyone could consider for this purpose is something like mine. Since I'm a university professor, my productivity is hard to quantify. Does my employer measure my output by the number of papers I publish? The number of talks I give? The hours of teaching I put in? The number of good ideas I have? It's also difficult to measure the quality of my work. For example, is this book any good, and by whose standards? Nor is the link between motivation and output direct or clear. Sometimes I might be highly motivated to find a particular answer to a question, but the concept I am working on is not the right one. Sometimes I might not be terribly motivated, but I stumble on a good research topic. The challenges with measuring my productivity are not unique to professors; in fact, they are common to most knowledge workers. Your productivity is likely to be as complex, if not more so, than mine to measure.

To test the effectiveness of different motivations, we needed to study a work environment in which employee output could be easily and accurately measured and where the tasks were more or less constant.

I lucked out when Guy Hochman, then a Duke postdoctoral fellow, introduced me to Liad Bareket, who worked in the HR department at Intel in Israel. Liad was interested in applying principles from social science to human motivation. Together with her team, we designed and implemented an experiment at their semiconductor production facility. This was exciting because we would get performance data for real working people, laboring at a task (assembling computer chips) that was both easily and accurately measurable.

At this semiconductor factory, the standard work cycle lasted eight days. Each workweek was composed of four days of twelve-hour shifts, followed by four days off. The factory managers set up a bonus structure to help motivate the chip makers, particularly on the first day of the work cycle. (The managers presumed that after four days off, the chip makers needed an extra boost to get their productivity mojo back.)

Their version of a bonus worked like this: Every morning, the manager informed the employees of their personal production target for the day. But on the first day of the work cycle, the manager also told them that if they reached that day's target, they would receive a cash bonus of 100 NIS (about $30) at the end of their shift. We thought that this structure was interesting, but we wanted to see how this approach stacked up against no bonus at all.

Usually, when we propose testing whether a company's existing approach truly produces the outcome its leaders expect, we don't encounter much enthusiasm. But, in this case, the Intel managers embraced the idea. This was encouraging, so we asked for another experimental condition: What if, rather than giving some employees a financial reward, we promised to deliver a delicious, family-sized pizza to their homes? This way, we argued, we not only would give them a gift, but we would also make them heroes in the eyes of their families.

The nice people at Intel liked the pizza idea. But the logistics turned out to be too complex for the HR folks. In the end, we had to compromise on a voucher for pizza. The voucher was not as wonderful as the pizza itself for the obvious reason that a piece of paper doesn't smell like mouthwatering, garlicky sauce, cheese, and freshly baked crust, and because the thought of eating a pizza tonight is much more immediately gratifying than a piece of paper representing a pizza in the future. But the voucher was sufficiently different from the $30 bonus that it was worth testing.

We did not stop there. Next, we asked for another condition. What if some people weren't offered a tangible reward at all, but instead received a text message from their boss saying, "Well done!" For the first time in my "let's try these ideas" history, the people in charge of compensation immediately agreed.

So, in total, we had four different conditions:

- Monetary bonus: On the first day of the work cycle, employees in this condition were greeted by the following message from their boss: "Good morning! If you reach or exceed X chips today, you'll receive 100 NIS in cash. Good luck!"

- Pizza voucher: This time, the boss wrote, "Good morning! If you reach or exceed X chips today, you'll receive a voucher for pizza. Good luck!"

- Compliment: In this condition, workers were greeted by a message that informed them that if they reached or exceeded their production target, they would get a text message from their boss telling them "Well done!"

- Control: In this case, chip makers received no note and were offered no bonus.

What Really Motivates Us?

Before I reveal the results, please pause for a moment and make a prediction. Do you think the tangible bonuses (money and pizza) improved the workers' performances over receiving nothing? And if so, which one of the two do you think inspired the highest level of performance? Or was it the simple "Well done!" that unleashed the highest level of motivation? Or was that message the worst, because it reminded employees that they were being asked to work for a kind word instead of a real bonus?

When I later asked a group of HR managers to predict the level of performance on the first day of the work cycle, they guessed that the cash would be the most motivating, followed by the pizza voucher. They thought the compliment would come in third place and the control condition dead last. Consistent with the intuitions of these HR managers, we indeed found that the cash, pizza, and a compliment all did better than the control condition. All three approaches increased motivation to a similar degree. But here was the surprise: the pizza voucher boosted productivity by 6.7 percent, almost identical to the 6.6 percent boost from the verbal reward. Of the three incentives, cash performed the worst, coming in slightly behind at 4.9 percent.

The results from the first day of the work cycle were clear. Any incentive is better than no incentive, and the types of incentives we used (money, pizza, and a compliment) weren't very different from one another. But this analysis focused only on the first day of the work cycle. What about the next three days of the work cycle? Would there be a residual effect of the bonus on performance?

This is where things got more interesting. On the second day of the work cycle, those in the money condition performed 13.2 percent *worse* than those in the control condition. It was as if they were saying to themselves, "Yesterday they paid me a bit extra, so I worked harder. But today they aren't offering me anything special, so I don't care." On the third day, the news was

THE DAY AFTER A COMPLIMENT

THE DAY AFTER A CASH BONUS

slightly less bleak; those in the money condition dropped their performance by only 6.2 percent relative to the control condition. By the fourth day, productivity had drifted back toward the baseline, with only a small decrease compared with the control condition (2.9 percent). Overall for the week, the monetary bonus condition resulted in a higher pay (the bonus) and a 6.5 percent drop in performance compared with no incentive at all.

What about the compliment and pizza conditions? As we mentioned earlier, performance in the compliment condition rose 6.6 percent on the first day of the work cycle. From there, it slowly drifted down toward the control condition over the next three days. And the pizza condition? It fell somewhere in the middle between the monetary bonus condition and the compliment condition. I suspect that if we offered a real pizza with a crispy crust and the smell of baked dough and melted cheese, we would have seen an effect similar to that of the compliment condition (perhaps with an even higher performance). And if a representative from Intel were to deliver the pizza personally, the employees would have probably been extra delighted. On the other hand, if Intel framed the pizza voucher in a more transactional way (for example, by mentioning its cost), its motivational power would have been more like the monetary bonus condition.

HEY, BOSS, WHAT ABOUT YOUR BONUS?
With these surprising results in mind, we told the top management at Intel about our findings. "Look," we said, "you thought that the monetary bonus would boost performance. But the data show that performance actually declined. You ended up paying a bonus and getting worse performance. Clearly, your intuitions about bonuses are not exactly on target. Why not let us test the effect of monetary bonuses throughout the company, including the bonuses for top management?" As you might have guessed, the executives had no interest in this research path.

Overlooking Intrinsic Motivation

One important lesson from our experiments at Intel is that different types of motivations don't add up in a simple way. In particular, adding money to the equation can backfire and make people *less* driven. We often assume people work for pay, and that more compensation will translate into greater output. Furthermore, I suspect that we hold this belief to an even larger extent when it comes to professions requiring significant physical labor and repetitive performance, with few demands for creativity. But at the semiconductor factory, which largely involved physical labor, this was clearly not the case. Instead, we saw that monetary bonuses resulted in the sharpest decrease in productivity, while rewarding people's performance with a compliment increased engagement even on the days when there was no bonus. These results suggest that there is a lot more to work than merely the opportunity to earn money in exchange for labor.

If you think broadly about these findings, it seems that we don't experience our work in day-to-day transactional terms. We don't measure our lives out in coffee spoons, as T. S. Eliot wrote, even in the most quotidian work. Instead, we think and behave on a longer time scale, which means that managers need to take into account (and measure) not only the direct effect of different incentives but also their delayed and enduring outcomes. The more a company can offer employees opportunities for meaning and connection, the harder those employees are likely to work and the more enduring their loyalty is likely to be.

Given that we have all been involved in many different types of tasks throughout our lifetimes, why can't we accurately understand and predict the effects of money on motivation? Are we that blind to our own experiences?

In a fascinating set of studies, Kaitlin Woolley and Ayelet Fishbach (both at the University of Chicago) measured the importance of intrinsic factors (the degree to which we are engaged in a task for its pure enjoyment) and the importance of extrinsic factors (how much we get paid).[14] Kaitlin and Ayelet conducted a variety of experiments at a gym to compare two types of motivations: intrinsic motivation linked to the experience itself (such as having a heart-pumping, stress-relieving workout) and extrinsic motivation linked to the outcome of finishing a task (such as improved health from working out). They found that when people were engaging in an activity (such as exercising), they cared most about intrinsic elements such as having a positive experience running on a treadmill or lifting weights. On the other hand, the researchers found that when people were *planning* to go to the gym, they cared most about extrinsic elements such as finishing the activity, getting healthier, and getting paid for their time.

In short, these findings suggest that when we are in the midst of a task, we focus on the inherent joy of the task, but when we think about the same task in advance, we overfocus on the extrinsic motivators, such as payment and bonuses. This is why we are not good predictors of what will motivate us and what will crush our motivation. This inability to intuit what will make us happy at work is sad. If you are a new college graduate considering your options, you might go for the high-paying job at a bank instead of pursuing your dream career as a jazz musician. Certainly, you will be able to afford more stuff and a nicer apartment if you take the bank job, but as you mull over these two options, are you overestimating the extrinsic motivators and underestimating the intrinsic joy of work?

DON'T OFFER MONEY TO MOM
Motivation can also be deeply influenced, both positively and negatively, by social norms. The cash bonus in our experiment at the semiconductor factory reflected market norms (a direct exchange of money for labor), leaving little room for caring and goodwill. The verbal "Well done!" followed the lines of social norms, which are essentially about gratitude, reciprocity, and the long-term relationship between employee and employer. In the

middle was the voucher, which operated more like a gift—it had some recognizable value, but it also conveyed some social ties and thoughtfulness.

In my book *Predictably Irrational*, I gave the following example to illustrate how money can have a negative effect on social norms (and apologies in advance to those of you who have already heard this one and remember it[15]):

> You are at your mother-in-law's house for Thanksgiving dinner, and what a sumptuous spread she has put on the table for you! The turkey is roasted to a golden brown; the stuffing is homemade and exactly the way you like it. Your kids are delighted: the sweet potatoes are crowned with marshmallows. And your wife is flattered that your in-laws chose her favorite recipe for pumpkin pie for dessert.
>
> The festivities continue into the late afternoon. You loosen your belt and sip a glass of wine. Gazing fondly across the table at your mother-in-law, you rise to your feet and pull out your wallet. "Mom, for all the love you've put into this, how much do I owe you?" you say sincerely. As silence descends on the gathering, you wave a handful of bills. "Do you think three hundred dollars will do it? No, wait, I should give you four hundred!"
>
> This is not a picture that Norman Rockwell would have painted. A glass of wine falls over. Your mother-in-law stands up red-faced, your sister-in-law shoots you an angry look, and your niece bursts into tears. Next year's Thanksgiving celebration, it seems, may be a frozen dinner in front of the television set.

This example illustrates that when we are motivated by social considerations, adding money to the mix can decrease the overall motivation and goodwill. Take dating, for example: A guy takes a girl out for dinner, a movie, and drinks, and he pays the bills. As they walk to her apartment, he thinks about his chances of getting a passionate good-night kiss, and just before leaning to kiss her, he casually mentions how much this evening has cost him. How likely is it that the evening will end well for him? There are some experiments that we don't need to run in order to know the outcome, and this is likely one. The moment we add money as a motivator in romantic relationships, only bad things can come of it.

The Power of Relationships

In the complex motivation equation, it's also important to realize that work is not zero-sum. Let's say I run a widget factory and you work for me. Each widget costs $3. For every unit you make, I pay you $1 and the business gets $2 (of which I receive a big percentage as the owner and CEO). The more widgets you make, the more $1 bills you are paid, and the more money you and I (especially I) make. Of course, if I pay you less—let's say 25 cents—I get even more money. This is how we usually think about the workplace. The metaphorical pie (i.e., our share of dollars) is assumed to be fixed, and, as a result, there is a deep conflict between business owners and workers, because when one makes more, the others make less.

We have the opposite metaphor when it comes to social relationships. When we're not at work, we don't consider most relationships to be in the fixed-pie category. Instead, most of our relationships fall into an expanding-pie category. We don't assume that if we receive more love from our parents, our spouse, or our kids, that we will give less of it in return. In fact, if we invest little love in a relationship, the bond will be fragile and we won't derive very much from it. But if we invest fully, we experience a stronger relationship. In the motivation equation, love in its various forms builds upon itself. When partners are in a successful relationship, each strengthens the other, and everyone in their circle benefits.

Applying this pie-expanding mind-set to the workplace implies that instead of relying only on money as an incentive, we need to expand our scope and examine other motivational forces—ones that provide a greater sense of meaning and connection to work. As people feel connected, challenged, and engaged; as they feel more trusted and autonomous; and as they get more recognition for their efforts, the total amount of motivation, joy, and output for everyone grows much larger.

Importantly, it is not that hard to create the conditions for pie expansion. Even doing something as small as lightening the collective mood can build motivation at work. In a lovely study, Sigal Barsad divided her students into many small groups and had each group play roles in an imaginary "salary committee" that had to determine how to balance a limited share of the company's funds against getting the most from their employees.[16] Unbeknownst to the students, Sigal asked an actor (a "confederate") to join the committee as well. The confederate played his role in one of four different moods. In some cases, he displayed "cheerful enthusiasm." In others, he radiated "serene warmth." In yet other cases, he showed "hostile irritability," and for the final type of performance, he portrayed "depressed sluggishness." The results showed that the actor's mood made a difference in all kinds of ways. The groups in which the confederate was cheerfully enthusiastic or serenely warm displayed more cooperation and less interpersonal conflict, performed better on their main task, and distributed raises more fairly than the groups in which the actor displayed negative emotions.

And while the behavior of the acting student influenced the behavior of the group, this was again a case where intuitions fail. When researchers asked the students why they thought that their groups performed as they did, the students did not point to the group dynamic as an important factor. They had no appreciation of the magnitude of the difference that positive social forces can play and how miserable we can become when we get exposed to negative social forces. The larger lesson here is that we can help our friends, our coworkers, our employees, and ourselves when we remember that love and caring matter.

The Joy of Long-term Relationships

How long does human connection have to last to deliver its boost to motivation? Imagine you wake up next to your significant other in the morning, feeling the glow of love. As you stretch, you say: "So, my darling, do you want to renew our relationship vows for another day?" Your significant other says,

"Sure," and then you both get up, shower, go to work, come home to dinner, go to bed, make love, and wake up the following morning. Then you ask the same question again. If you lived in this sort of day-by-day romantic life, what would your mutual investment in your relationship be like? Most likely not that much. When we decide to marry someone "for better, for worse; for richer, for poorer; in sickness and in health," we're committing not for the day, week, month, or year, but for as long you both shall live, or at least as long as possible.

Or let's say you procure a nice apartment in Midtown Manhattan overlooking Central Park. You wake up in the morning with the sun streaming through the window, pour yourself a steaming cup of coffee, and ask yourself, "Do I want to stay in this beautiful apartment another day?" In such circumstances, you would hardly bother painting the bathroom, fixing a crack in the molding, or investing money in furniture and plants. You might as well live in a hotel.

The point is that good relationships aren't transactional; our need for connectedness anchors them on a longer time scale. You won't bother putting a lot of energy into a short-term relationship, whether with a romantic partner, employer, colleague, or apartment. But if you think of that relationship as a long-term investment, then you will be motivated to deposit more of your love, trust, energy, and time. This sense of investment is the basis of the marriage vow, and it is the basis of true dedication and loyalty in the workplace. In the world of workplaces, the relationship between universities and professors is as good as it gets. Universities, on their side, give professors tenure, and with this lifetime commitment, professors look at the university with deep trust and a long-term view.

How can businesses that don't have lifelong tenure systems give commitment to and get commitment from their employees? There are a lot of things that we can do to communicate a sense of long-term commitment: we can invest in employees' education, provide them with health benefits that clearly communicate a commitment to a joint healthy future, invest in their well-being both within and outside of work, invest in their personal growth, and provide them with a path for promotion and development within the company. These kinds of actions don't guarantee long-term employment (in the same way that marriage does not guarantee that you will stay together until death do you part), but they certainly change the time frame of the commitment to a longer one.

From Marx to Smith and Back

One of the early thinkers about the meaning of labor in the modern world was Karl Marx. In 1844, Marx wrote about what he called "the alienation of labor," which described a situation in which someone works on a small sub-task, in a small part of a larger enterprise. Like the worker in Adam Smith's pin factory, the laborer has no idea what his project is all about. He doesn't understand how his work fits in with the enterprise as a whole. It is unclear to him who will use the product he makes, and he generally feels no connection to the organization, the project, the end user, or the outcome.

It is clear that Adam Smith and Karl Marx had very different understandings of the nature of productivity. Smith assumed that management could change the structure of the workplace and achieve more efficiency without sacrificing human motivation. Marx, on the other hand, assumed that the efficiency gained from breaking tasks into components would come at the expense of human motivation. Which perspective is correct?

As is often the case in deep philosophical debates, each was correct on some level. Obviously, there are all kinds of efficiency gains to be had by breaking tasks into components. At the same time, as our research has shown, getting people to care deeply about their jobs, by adding meaning, personal investment, and connection, can create substantial benefits for both employees and employers. Work quality, morale, and productivity all improve.

While both perspectives contain important truths, I believe that in an increasingly knowledge-based economy, it's becoming increasingly important to design organizations along Marx's point of view. In the knowledge economy, the workplace relies heavily on trust, engagement, and goodwill—and as the autonomy of each person in the organization increases, so does the importance of making everyone feel deeply connected to the enterprise.

Reflecting on my relationship with Duke University, I think of myself as someone who benefits from a win-win relationship. My work as a university professor and researcher is my job, but it is also my hobby and, to a large degree, my identity and my life. Aside from the few moments when I sneeze and when I have an orgasm, I am constantly thinking about human nature. I think about what we know and don't know about ourselves; about how to make things better; and about new and more interesting experiments that might shine some light on human behavior.

I love this life, and it is hard for me to think about what I would do if I stopped being a professor. The benefits to my employer are clear: Duke gets a highly dedicated employee who is motivated to advance the university's mission. And the benefits to me are clear: I love going to work; I love working with my students and collaborators; I take great pride in our research findings; and I get extra delight when our insights are applied in the real world. But perhaps most important, I feel that the work I do can have some long-lasting impact on how we go about our lives.

I'm not a Marxist by political and definitional standards, but I will say this: When people are not able to focus on the larger meaning of their labor, they are more or less stuck in the modern equivalent of a pin factory. Granted, developing a workplace that is centered on meaning is not easy. It is certainly more complex than the current efficiency-based model of breaking tasks into components, departments, job specialties, and sub-organizations. But in an era in which knowledge work is prized and creativity arguably matters far more than efficiency, Marx's view on alienation, connection, and control should be baked more directly into the DNA of modern organizations. To me, the lesson from our research on motivation seems very clear. As we become meaningfully engaged with our work, we become both happier and more productive—a win-win situation if there ever was one.

The Value of Goodwill

Imagine that all jobs could be characterized along two dimensions: the "countable" dimension comprises that which is concrete, well defined, and easily measurable (number of pins made, chips created, gadgets sold, and so on), while the "uncountable" dimension is somewhat ill defined and difficult to measure (improving a process, helping others, thinking brilliant thoughts, etc.). Of course, some jobs are more countable than others.

When organizations attempt to create their compensation schemes, the first mistake they often make, as followers of the pin-factory doctrine, is to overemphasize the countable dimension. Following the principle of looking for your keys under the street lamp, managers are drawn to the subset of tasks that are easily measurable. As a consequence, they overemphasize those parts of the job and divert attention and effort away from the uncountable dimension.

The second mistake managers often make is to treat the uncountable dimension as if it were easily countable. In fact, reducing labor to something simplistic and countable often misses the heart of motivation altogether. How many times are employees judged on the number of reports they have written, rather than on the quality of the work in the reports themselves?

Here's another case in point: Before I became a professor at Duke University, I taught at MIT. The teaching requirement at this amazing institution was based on a point system. Professors were supposed to teach 112 points, which we earned through a combination of time in the classroom, the number of students we taught, the number of hours the students worked, the overall class load, and so on. As it turned out, it was fairly easy to game the system and focus on research. In fact, I was so good at this that I managed to teach one large class a year, composed of twelve three-hour sessions (yes, thirty-six hours of classroom teaching a year).

The sad point is that I enjoy teaching. And some students enjoyed my classes. The problem was that the measurement system directed me to work my hardest to try to minimize teaching time and compelled me to figure out how I could teach as little as possible.

In setting up the point system this way, the designers of this incentive system (no doubt having nothing but good intentions) chase away the most important ingredients of the uncountable dimension: basic trust and goodwill. From the earliest stages of development, we learn that we can earn trust and goodwill by extending the same thing to our parents and others. If we smile, they smile; if we offer them some of our soggy animal cookie, they give us a crisper animal cookie. As adults, when we buy something on credit, the creditor is extending goodwill to us, and, in return, we pay the bill on time. Such reciprocity is the foundation of a well-functioning society.

The exchange of trust and goodwill is an important and inherent part of human motivation. If you try to reflect on the role of trust in your own life, it should become apparent how many of our everyday interactions involve trust. We trust that the people who work with us will not steal our stuff and will respect our privacy, that the people working at the cafeteria will take

HOW MONETARY INCENTIVES WORK:

HOW NONMONETARY INCENTIVES WORK:

YOUR ENJOYMENT POWERS THIS RIDE CONTINUOUSLY

care to make sure that the food we eat is healthy and not spoiled. We trust that the babysitter we hire will take good care of our children. We trust that the neighbor isn't going to steal our mail, break into our house, or kill the dog. A society without trust isn't a society: it's a collection of people who are continuously afraid of each other.

Trust and goodwill also inspires us to step out of our standard job requirements in order to excel and innovate. (If you like cooking, you can think of goodwill in culinary terms: it's the extraordinary spice that makes an ordinary dish so special, flavorful, and meaningful.) If you stop and consider your job for a few minutes, you will probably come up with many ways in which the exchange of trust and goodwill influences your desire to deliver real progress. Just think about all the times you stayed late at the office, answered emails while on vacation, helped a colleague on a project unrelated to your work, or thought about work-related questions on the weekend.

Unfortunately, there are many ways to kill trust and goodwill. The simplest is to pay people directly for their performance. Imagine, for example, that you worked for me and I asked you to stay late three times over the next week to help complete a project ahead of deadline. At the end of the week, you will have not seen your family but will have come close to a caffeine overdose. As an expression of my gratitude I present you with one of two rewards. In option one, I tell you how much your extra hard work meant to me. I give you a warm and sincere hug and invite you and your family to dinner. In option two, I tell you that I have calculated your marginal contribution to the company's bottom line, it totaled $27,800, and I tell you that I will give you a bonus of 5 percent of this amount ($1,390). Which scenario is more likely to maximize your goodwill toward the company and me, not just on that day, but moving forward? Which will inspire you to push extra hard to meet the next deadline?

As the compliment condition at Intel and our other experiments on social norms show, my thanks, hug, and our family dinner would make all the difference in your feelings of current and future engagement. The bonus, however, would put a numerical value on something that wasn't countable to begin with: your commitment. And while you might appreciate the cash, the next time I ask you to help me with a deadline, you will most likely ask "How much?"

Let's Kill the Lawyers[17]

Speaking of ruining trust and goodwill, let's take a look at legal contracts. Now, in many cases contracts are absolutely necessary, but the way they are created, the language used, and their terms can easily destroy trust and goodwill.

Not long ago, I spent some time with a big company that does a lot of business with various suppliers. In the early days, the woman who founded the company would meet with her suppliers and confirm agreements with a handshake. Then the company grew. With that growth came lawyers and official contracts. These lawyers tried to plan for all kinds of low-probability events: what if the suppliers produced things that triggered allergies, caught on fire, were found to be toxic, or changed color in storage?

These potential events may have been reasonable topics of

discussion, but when the lawyers insisted on including them as explicit items in contracts, they came across as accusations. The implication appeared to be that the suppliers were both incompetent and uncaring. Of course, it was the lawyers' job to anticipate all kinds of unlikely events, but these contracts also destroyed any goodwill. After holding these discussion (accusation) sessions with their suppliers, the old-timers at the company told me their relationships had become poisoned. If the company ever needed something beyond what was included in the original contract (a quicker delivery time or a change in quantity, for example), suppliers took it as an opportunity to charge more. The contracts were ironclad, but what the company gained in legalese it lost in goodwill.

Legal mangling, of course, is not limited to the workplace. Consider the story of a single female friend of mine (I'll call her "Anne") and her gay male next-door neighbor ("Rob"). Anne and Rob were both single, in their late thirties, and enjoying their lives in Manhattan. Both had good jobs and ample resources. But they each realized they wanted to have a child.

Anne and Rob came up with a simple, ingenious plan that would let them maintain their mutual independence while also having a family. They would have a child together using in vitro fertilization (IVF). They were good friends. They enjoyed long walks and meals together, and they visualized how their friendship would continue and grow stronger with a cute kid swinging in between them. Sharing a child, while remaining independent, would let them enjoy the best of both family and single life.

Under this perfect arrangement, Anne and Rob would each

have custody for a few days a week and enjoy their own single lives on the other days. They would each surrender sleep for a few days a week to care for the baby, but they would be free otherwise. They could have lovers of their choice but still enjoy the warmth and love of shared parenthood. They lived next door to each other, so the kid would have two loving homes. In contrast to most couples who plan to stay together and are caught by surprise when things don't work out, Anne and Rob would start their family as separated parents. "Wouldn't it be much better," Anne asked me, "for the kid to have a healthy separation from the start instead of the high probability of a bitter divorce?" Anne and Rob wondered if the whole institution of marriage was passé. They figured that one day, when we are in a more enlightened era, everyone will approach the family structure this way.

They were ready to start the IVF process when a friend suggested that they first see a family lawyer to ensure that their agreement was legally solid. The lawyer asked Anne and Rob questions about their backgrounds—their childhoods, families, current lives, work, hobbies, and incomes. Next, he presented them with a set of dilemmas that they might face as a family. How would they resolve simple conflicts if, for example, days of custody needed to be changed at the last moment because of a sickness, a date, or a work trip? Working with the lawyer, Anne and Rob tried to flesh out a contract to sort out these potentialities.

Next, the lawyer asked them to think about more complex conflicts: What if they disagreed about what time the child should go to bed, the amount of TV time, or the importance of doing homework? What if one wanted to send the kid to a private school and the other didn't want to or couldn't afford it? What if one of them got a significant promotion at work or had to move to a new city or country? Would they be allowed to move? Would the other move as well?

Under the lawyer's guidance, Anne and Rob tried to figure out what they would do. They debated these hypothetical cases with as much intensity and passion as if they were real. They soon found themselves disagreeing strongly and resenting each other's stubbornness. It became clear that they were not going to create a new ideal family. Instead, they wound up hating each other. They haven't spoken since.

The perspective on Anne and Rob's dilemma is very different when you think of the family as a single unified entity and not as a contractual agreement between separate individuals. In a long-term relationship in which people are committed to each other and not just to their child, there is an implicit understanding that ties the individuals to common goals. Committed couples are willing to give up something now for benefits in the future ("I will slow down my career path for a few years to support yours") and are willing to put their own preferences on the back burner for the benefit of the family unit as a whole ("I love this city, but it is better for all of us if we move"). The basic lesson is that when we are committed and think long-term, we largely put aside our own agenda for the good of the family, and when we do so, wonderful things can occur.

Nourishing Goodwill

It seems self-evident that our family, social, and professional lives depend to a large degree on goodwill. But while we usually recognize the importance of goodwill in our romantic and social relationships, we don't seem to appreciate its role in the workplace to the same degree. In fact, we often take actions that erode or even crush goodwill. At Intel, for example, we saw how paying people bonuses, in a shortsighted way, killed their motivation. Instead of understanding the crucial importance of human connection, companies create rules and lists of punishments. But these approaches only work in the short-term and only when we are able to specify all of the exact potential outcomes.

To foster goodwill at work, companies need to make it a core value, across the company. One of the most gallant efforts to reinforce goodwill came from Doug Conant, Campbell Soup Company's former CEO, who handwrote thank-you notes to people whose acts of goodwill reached his ears or his inbox. By the time he left the company, he'd written more than thirty thousand such notes.[18] The net-net is this: It is relatively easy to create goodwill. All we need is an encouraging word here and there, a gift from time to time, and a sincere look in the eyes. But we also need to keep in mind that goodwill is fragile. Supporting it is easy, but destroying it is even easier.

4 On Death, Relationships, and Meaning

The crazy urge for symbolic immortality, and how love conquers all

Xin Zhui isn't much to look at now. Her skin sags. Her arms, hands, and legs are ridden with valleys of wrinkles. Her eyes are sunken. Her limbs are still flexible, though she has a terrible back—a disc in her spine is fused. She has clogged coronary arteries as well as gallstones, probably the result of having eaten too much high-calorie, fatty food.

Yet despite all of her ailments and her astonishing age, you can still see some vestiges of Xin Zhui's former beauty. Her hands and feet are well formed. She still has the high cheekbones of her youth, and tiny, shell-like ears. Her tongue sticks out between her lips, which gives her a vaguely amused expression, as if she is about to lick an ice cream cone. She seems so alive. There's that hair—a full head of indigo. And her toes still invite a pink-polish pedicure. What beauty secret is this lady hanging on to?

There is no question that Xin Zhui (aka Lady Dai, aka the "Botox Babe" of anthropologists) is pretty good-looking for a woman who is more than 2,100 years old.

When she was thirty, Xin Zhui was most likely nothing less than spectacular. She had wide-set, intelligent, imperious, almond-shaped eyes, full lips, and beautiful coloring.[19] As the perfect trophy wife of a marquis, she led a life of bored luxury; with everything available to her, she had precious little to do. So she soaked herself in every possible comfort. Gorgeous, spoiled, and gluttonous, Lady Dai was her own ancient Han Dynasty version of Marie Antoinette or Leona Helmsley.[20]

Aside from being pampered, how else did Lady Dai spend her time? Apparently, she spent it thinking about the wonderful afterlife she would have in her next big, beautiful, amply appointed house. And her plan, years in the making, was carried out perfectly. When she finally breathed her last—evidently from heart disease, at the then-old age of fifty—Lady Dai's servants doused her body in a mildly acidic, reddish liquid of mysterious origin, which anthropologists think might have been considered an elixir of immortality during her time.

They then swaddled her in twenty layers of bacteria-suffocating silk and encased her in a small coffin, which they placed inside another coffin, and another one, and another one, like Russian nesting dolls. The final and huge exterior coffin was made of special wood brought from more than a thousand miles away.

She was discovered in 1971, centuries after her death, entombed fifty feet below the earth in a chamber that held her huge sarcophagus. She was buried under five tons of charcoal and earth, which effectively vacuum sealed her tomb. To some extent, Lady Dai did achieve immortality, because she is the best-preserved mummy ever discovered. According to the medical examiners, all her organs, including her brain, were found to be intact, including some of the red, albeit dry, type A blood in her veins.

Buried with her was everything this gluttonous lady needed, including beautiful lacquer dinnerware and thirty bamboo caskets of fruit, soybeans, swans, dogs, pheasants, and pigs on which she loved to feast.[21] It was a bounteous supply, intended to last her another lifetime.

Symbolic Immortality and the Need for Meaning

Like Lady Dai, people in power across the ages and cultures all over the globe have taken measures to go on living after death. In ancient Egypt, for example, royal tombs were elaborately designed and laden with provisions—clothing, furniture, toiletries, food, and drinks—for sustenance in the afterlife. But the ancient custom of burying people with grave goods has never completely, ahem, died out. In 1899, a man named Reuben John Smith had himself entombed sitting on a brand-new leather chair with a checkerboard in his lap (and the key to the tomb in his pocket). In 2005, a Manhattan lawyer named John Jacobs was buried with his active cell phone so that his wife could call him.[22] And when a California socialite named Sandra Ilene West died in 1977, she was interred dressed in a lace nightgown, in her 1964 Ferrari.[23]

The question, of course, is why do people bother? Spending money on fancy cars, expensive cosmetics, lavish food and wine while one is alive might seem wasteful, but at least we get to enjoy them. Why bother burying ourselves in a Ferrari or carrying an active cell phone into the grave? What kinds of benefits might we possibly derive from these products when we're dead?

This kind of investment might make sense if you believe that any material goods left at the tomb will stay fresh and be perfectly useful when you wake from death. But what about those who don't believe they will go on living to enjoy their lovely, tangible possessions? The non-afterlife-believers also hold on to the hope that something will live on after death—their DNA in the form of their children and/or their accomplishments and contributions. Whether you believe in the literal kind of immortality or not, it seems that we all feel a craving for some kind of afterlife—that we will be remembered after we're gone, even if all that remains of us is a lonely, symbolic grave marker that attests to the fact that we were once a living, breathing, and beloved human being.

How deep is this need for symbolic immortality? Before you answer this question, ask yourself how you would feel if everything you did throughout your life was erased from the face of the earth the moment you died. What if you knew, from the moment that you started understanding the world, that everything you wrote, created, every memory of you, and every thought that others had about you would simply disappear without a trace upon your death? How would this knowledge influence your daily life? Would you wake up every morning feeling excited to go to work, to create, to take care of your family, and so on? I'm just beginning to do some research on these questions, but so far it seems clear that many of our motivations are based on a horizon longer than our lifetimes and that, in its absence, much of our motivation would be crushed.

Naomi's Will

In our thinking about death, our desire for meaning can morph into all kinds of urges, strange beliefs, emotions, and motivations that at first seem to make no rational sense. For example, why should it matter so much what other people think about us after we're dead?

Consider wills, for example. I once knew a wealthy, aging widow with a heart problem—let's call her Naomi. Naomi had

two sons. Her older, fifty-something son, "Ben," was a tall, strong, former semipro tennis player and upright citizen. He had been a straight-A student in college and had gone on to have an illustrious legal career and a beautiful, happy family. The younger son, "Jake," had been a lifelong rebel. A jazz musician in his mid-forties, Jake barely eked out a living and had never settled down.

Naomi often asked Jake, "Why can't you be more like your

brother?" The more she berated him, made suggestions for improving himself, and compared him to Ben, the angrier and more withdrawn Jake became. Eventually he barely spoke to her.

Now, imagine Naomi drawing up her will, weighing what she wants to leave her sons. Does she leave most of her fortune to Ben, the good son with the lovely family? Does she divide it equally between the two of them? Does she leave most of it to Jake, the less-than-wonderful son, in hopes that he feels grateful and perhaps turns his life around? Does she leave most of it to her favorite charity? What would you do if you were Naomi?

Before you answer, let's step back for a moment and think about wills. If you wanted to experience a tangible benefit from giving away your fortune, wouldn't you do it while you were still alive so that you could enjoy seeing firsthand the effects of your generosity? Maybe you could reconcile with your estranged son, or enjoy the gratitude of both children, or enjoy helping your favorite charity expand its impact? After you're dead, it will be much harder for you to enjoy any of the outcomes of your wonderful actions. When you look at giving this way, it becomes clear that waiting until you are no longer around to give your money is, at its core, pretty irrational.

After Naomi died of a heart attack, Ben dutifully arranged a sumptuous funeral to which Jake never bothered to show up, insulting the entire extended family.

So how do you think Naomi distributed her fortune?

In her will, she bequeathed $25,000 and some sentimental

items to Ben. She gave another $25,000 to her favorite charity. She left the rest of her substantial fortune to Jake—noting that she regretted not having valued him enough during her lifetime. She wanted to make up with him and for him to feel more loved and appreciated—but she did it in a way that moved their relationship forward only after she died.

Our Strange Postmortem Predilections

Naomi's desire for an intangible postmortem reconciliation with Jake may seem odd, but her example is run-of-the-mill compared to some other attempts at post-death connections. One such man, Solomon Sandborn, asked in his will that his skin be stripped from his corpse and made into two drums and that his friend Warren Simpson would play "Yankee Doodle" on these skin drums at Bunker Hill on the 17th of June every year, in commemoration of the Revolutionary War battle fought there.

A man named Samuel Bratt, whose wife had no doubt badgered him about his smoking, bequeathed her £333,000 under the condition that she smoke five cigars a day. The German poet Heinrich Heine displayed similar feelings about his wife: he left his estate to her on the condition that she remarry to ensure that "there would be at least one man to regret my death."[24] Some people leave fortunes to their animals: the ultra-wealthy Leona Helmsley, for example, left nothing to two of her grandchildren but bequeathed $12 million to her Maltese, who had no idea how to spend it (though the dog's caretaker undoubtedly took the dog out to fantastic restaurants).

It is hard to tell whether Naomi, Samuel Bratt, Heinrich Heine, Leona Helmsley, and many others who have used their wills to control their "loved ones" after death believed in some kind of tangible afterlife reward or not. But the choices they made while alive about their afterlives show how the prospect of death motivated them in all kinds of strange ways.

One way to understand post-life motivations is by examining funerals. Because they symbolize a transition between life and death, they provide a magnifying glass with which to examine the way we view and make decisions about the afterlife. Funerals in Soweto and other poor communities in Africa, for example, can cost a substantial amount of the family's yearly household income—building up the deceased's reputation but destroying the wealth of the living relatives. In the United States, too, spending on funerals is a common path to financial ruin. One sad example is a story I recently heard about a couple, both with serious health issues and no money. When the wife passed away, her husband, who loved her so much, borrowed money to pay for a nice casket and embalming so that her beautiful face could be viewed at the funeral. A few hours later, they cremated her body, and a few months later, the husband went bankrupt.

In our studies on funerals, we found that grieving people don't consider money as much when planning funerals. People are willing to spend more on the accoutrements of a funeral (coffin, flowers, and service) for a loved one than they would choose for themselves, even though they realize that the loved one would have counseled them to spend their money more wisely. And this overspending is not limited to people who have money to spare. The point is that we, the living, are driven by a range of motivations, including the way we want to think about the dead, their role in our lives, our role in their lives, and the prospect of our own mortality. From this perspective, closely examining funerals gives us some interesting insights on the drive for literal and symbolic immortality, and the kinds of motivations that influence us more generally, including caring about others, helping, making amends, and finding meaning.

Observing funerals and the rituals around them makes it clear that we have a deep need for "symbolic immortality." At either a conscious or unconscious level, we want to outlast our physical life and to be remembered through the things we leave behind us—our children or our achievements. This is why wealthy individuals start charitable foundations and put their names on buildings; why starving artists draw and write; why graffiti artists paint on underground walls; why children carve their names in rocks and trees; why Michelangelo painted on the ceilings of chapels; why athletes work so hard to break records; and even why some people eat hundreds of hot dogs at a sitting, just to get their names in the Guinness World Records.

Our motivation to leave a legacy is powerful and interesting in its own right, but maybe more than any other type of motivation, it provides us a window into the complexity and multiplicity of the elements in our motivation equation—an equation that we are just starting to uncover, appreciate, and understand.

The Answer to the Ultimate Question

The mystery of motivation, in summary

In *The Hitchhiker's Guide to the Galaxy*, Douglas Adams describes the search for the "Answer to the Ultimate Question of Life, the Universe, and Everything." To get this answer, a specially built supercomputer called Deep Thought spent 7.5 million years toiling away. Here's the passage from the book:

> "Good Morning," said Deep Thought at last.
>
> "Er . . . good morning, O Deep Thought," said Loonquawl nervously, "do you have . . . er, that is . . ."
>
> "An Answer for you?" interrupted Deep Thought majestically. "Yes, I have."
>
> The two men shivered with expectancy. Their waiting had not been in vain.
>
> "There really is one?" breathed Phouchg.
>
> "There really is one," confirmed Deep Thought.
>
> "To Everything? To the great Question of Life, the Universe and everything?"
>
> "Yes."
>
> Both of the men had been trained for this moment, their lives had been a preparation for it, they had been selected at birth as those who would witness the answer, but even so they found themselves gasping and squirming like excited children.

"And you're ready to give it to us?" urged Loonquawl.

"I am."

"Now?"

"Now," said Deep Thought.

They both licked their dry lips.

"Though I don't think," added Deep Thought, "that you're going to like it."

"Doesn't matter!" said Phouchg. "We must know it! Now!"

"Now?" inquired Deep Thought.

"Yes! Now . . ."

"All right," said the computer, and settled into silence again. The two men fidgeted. The tension was unbearable.

"You're really not going to like it," observed Deep Thought.

"Tell us!"

"All right," said Deep Thought. "The Answer to the Great Question . . ."

"Yes . . . !"

"Of Life, the Universe and Everything . . ." said Deep Thought.

"Yes . . . !"

"Is . . ." said Deep Thought, and paused.

"Yes . . . !"

"Is . . ."

"Yes . . . !!! . . .?"

"Forty-two," said Deep Thought, with infinite majesty and calm.[25]

As Deep Thought provided 42 as the Answer to the Ultimate
Question of Life, the Universe, and Everything, it also
pointed out that the answer is meaningless because it was
never clear what the Question was. When asked to produce
"the Ultimate Question," Deep Thought said that it could not;
however, it could help to design an even more powerful computer that, after running for ten million years, would be able
to provide the question. In the story, Planet Earth turns out to
be this more powerful computer.

This same logic applies to the question of motivation:
It is such a general and large question that it encompasses
almost every aspect of human endeavor and drive. Because
the question of motivation is so complex, exploring it is like
being lost in the Amazon jungle without a map. We can't
provide a single answer or perspective to motivation as a
whole, and even if we could, doing so would probably take an
infinitely long time. After all, philosophers, psychologists,
crime novelists, and many, many others have struggled with
the question of motivation, and so far we have only fumbled
our way toward 42.

As we've seen, the story of motivation isn't at all straight-
forward. Rather, it is intricate and mysterious. In addition
to our general appreciation for the complexity of human
motivation, what specific lessons have we learned? Among all
of the motivating forces in the world, it turns out that money
isn't the simple, great motivator most of us assume it to be. In
fact, sometimes it is a disincentive. We've also learned that,
at some point or another, we all become offenders against

(perhaps even killers of) human motivation when we ignore, criticize, disregard, or destroy the work of others.

We have also learned that we're much more driven by all kinds of intangible, emotional forces: the need to be recognized and to feel ownership; to feel a sense of accomplishment; to find the security of a long-term commitment and a sense of shared purpose. We want to feel as if our labor and lives matter in some way, even after death.

To motivate ourselves and others successfully, we need to provide a sense of connection and meaning—remembering that meaning is not always synonymous with personal happiness. Arguably, the most powerful motivator in the world is our connection to others. I remember a teenager named Sarah, a patient for a short time in the burn unit of the hospital where I was treated. After a breakup from her boyfriend, Sarah tried to commit suicide by slitting her wrists and rubbing Ajax, a toxic cleanser, into the wounds. When she was well enough to walk around, she began to visit other patients on the ward—patients who were in much worse shape, with deeper and more extensive wounds. She went from room to room offering us water, telling us stories, chatting with us, and generally brightening the mood of that terrible place. In seeing how lucky she was compared to the rest of us, and how much we all appreciated her visits, she quickly got out of her romantic melancholy.

During World War II, the great moral philosopher Victor Frankl discovered how a sense of connection to his beloved helped him survive a Nazi death camp. One night as he and fellow prisoners were being marched through a dark forest, a fellow prisoner turned to him and whispered, "What if our wives could see us now?" Frankl looked up at the stars and thought of his own beloved wife's face. He heard the sound of her voice and felt her presence. That presence gave him the strength to live, even as people all around him died. Afterward, he went on to give the world a rich legacy of work, including *Man's Search for Meaning*, in which he included these words:

> For the first time in my life I saw the truth as it is set into song by so many poets, proclaimed as the final wisdom by so many thinkers. The truth—that Love, Meaning and Connection are the ultimate and highest goal to which man can aspire. Then I grasped the meaning of the greatest secret that human poetry and human thought and belief have to impart: The salvation of man is through love and in love.[26]

Ultimately, this book asks you—whether you're an executive, a parent, a salesperson, a teacher, a government official, or anyone else who seeks to motivate yourself or others—to think deeply and broadly about the effects of your approach. My hope is that by understanding some of the hidden forces of motivation, we will find it easier to deploy the positive, intangible drivers that affect us. After all, if a kind word can do wonders to impel people to do better, what other hidden treasures of energy, dedication, and commitment might we find if we only looked for them?

In the realm of physics, people have long dreamt of the possibility of getting something out of nothing—in other words, creating the "perpetual motion machine." Building a real perpetual motion machine is impossible, since it would violate the laws of thermodynamics. But when it comes to human motivation, we can have perpetual energy as long as we invest in a sense of connection, meaning, ownership, and long-term thinking. And if we correctly use these forces, the return on investment in human motivation will be immense.

We are certainly far from grasping the full complexity of motivation, but the journey to understand the thousands of strange and wonderful nuances beneath Motivation with a capital M is going to be exciting, interesting, important, and useful. And if we do it right, the journey will reveal the secrets of more productivity, love, and meaning. Now, that's motivating.

ACKNOWLEDGMENTS

Research is a community effort that depends on many colleagues and collaborators. Over the years, I have had the privilege to work with many smart, creative, generous individuals whom I also consider friends. The research described in this book is largely an outcome of their ingenuity and insight, while any mistakes and omissions are mine. Research is also driven by many helpers who work hard at the research process, and I want to thank the amazing group at the Center for Advanced Hindsight at Duke University.

My deepest thanks also go to my agent Jim Levine, my right and left hand Megan Hogerty, my writing sherpa Bronwyn Frycr, and my editor Michelle Quint. I also want thank all the individuals who so generously participate in our experiments. They help us get a slightly improved understanding of what we do wrong, what we do right, and how we can improve our sorry state. And finally, I have learned a great deal about meaning and satisfaction with the help of my lovely wife, Sumi, and our two kids, Amit and Neta. I know that I have a lot more to learn, and I promise to keep on trying.

NOTES

1   As long as you don't expect a simple answer to this question by the end of the book, we are going to be okay.

2   My father used to say that having very young kids at home is a sure way to get people to stay in the office longer.

3   Roy Baumeister, Kathleen Vohns, Jennifer Aaker, Emily Garbinsky, "Some Key Differences Between a Happy Life and a Meaningful Life," *Journal of Positive Psychology* (2013).

4   Dan Ariely, Emir Kamenica, and Drazen Prelec, "Man's Search for Meaning: The Case of Legos," *Journal of Economic Behavior & Organization* (2008).

5   Amy Adkins, "Majority of U.S. Employees Not Engaged Despite Gains in 2014," *Gallup*, January 28, 2015, http://www.gallup.com/poll/181289/majority-employees -not-engaged-despite-gains-2014.aspx.

6   Adam Smith, "An Inquiry into the Nature and Causes of the Wealth of Nations," http://geolib.com/smith.adam/won1-01.html.

7   John Maynard Keynes, *The General Theory of Employment, Interest and Money* (1936).

8   Michelle Park, "A History of the Cake Mix, the Invention That Redefined 'Baking,'" http://www.bonappetit.com/entertaining-style/pop-culture/article/ cake-mix-history.

9   Mike Norton, Daniel Mochon, and Dan Ariely "The IKEA Effect: When Labor Leads to Love," *Journal of Consumer Psychology* (2012).

Daniel Mochon, Mike Norton, and Dan Ariely, "Bolstering and Restoring Feelings of Competence via the IKEA Effect," *International Journal of Research in Marketing* (2012).

10   I wrote about this in *Irrationally Yours* (New York: HarperCollins, 2015).

11   Alex Shaw, Vivian Li, and Kristina Olson, "Children Apply Principles of Physical Ownership to Ownership of Ideas," *Cognitive Science* (2012).

12   Ibid.

13   Dan Ariely, Uri Gneezy, George Loewenstein, and Nina Mazar, "Large Stakes and Big Mistakes," *Review of Economic Studies* (2009).

14   Kaitlin Woolley and Ayelet Fishbach, "The Experience Matters More Than You Think: People Value Intrinsic Incentives More Inside Than Outside an Activity," *Journal of Personality and Social Psychology* (2015).

15   Dan Ariely, *Predictably Irrational* (New York: HarperCollins, 2008).

16   Sigal Bardas, "The Ripple Effect: Emotional Contagion and Its Effect on Group Behavior," *Administrative Science Quarterly* (2002).

17   William Shakespeare, *Henry VI,* part 2, act 4, scene 2, line 73.

18   Douglas R. Conant, "Secrets of Positive Feedback," *Harvard Business Review,* February 16, 2011, https://hbr.org/2011/02/secrets-of-positive-feedback/.

19   Eti Bonn-Muller, "China's Sleeping Beauty," *Archaeology*, April 10, 2009, http://www.archaeology.org/online/features/mawangdui/.

20   "Mawangdui," *Wikipedia*, last modified March 20, 2016, http://en.wikipedia.org/wiki/Mawangdui.

21   Sam Savage, "Meet the Lady Dai," *Red Orbit*, November 4, 2004, http://www.redorbit.com/news/health/100340/meet_the_lady_dai____of_145bc_/.

22   Liz Langley, "Toilets, Headless Bodies, and Other Weird Things People Get Buried With," *National Geographic*, November 7, 2013, http://voices.nationalgeographic.com/2013/11/07/toilets-headless-bodies-and-other-weird-things-people-get-buried-with/.

23   "5 People Buried with Strange Objects," *How Stuff Works: Entertainment,* http://entertainment.howstuffworks.com/5-people-buried-with-strange-objects.htm#page=4.

24   Matt Branham, "The Oddest Things Bequeathed in Dead People's Wills," November 24, 2014, http://www.mandatory.com/2014/11/24/the-oddest-things-bequeathed-in-dead-peoples-wills/.

Alex Mathews Blog, http://www.alexmathews.com/212/random/10-last-laughs-weird-wills-and-strange-legacies/.

25   Douglas Adams, *The Hitchhiker's Guide to the Galaxy* (New York: Del Rey Books, 1995).

26   Viktor Frankl, *Man's Search for Meaning* (New York: Simon & Schuster, Touchstone edition, 1959).

ABOUT THE AUTHOR

Dan Ariely is the James B. Duke Professor of Psychology & Behavioral Economics at Duke University. He is the founder and director of the Center for Advanced Hindsight, cocreator of the film documentary *(Dis)Honesty: The Truth About Lies*, and a three-time New York Times bestselling author. His books include *Predictably Irrational*, *The Upside of Irrationality*, *The Honest Truth About Dishonesty*, and *Irrationally Yours*.

He lives in Durham, North Carolina, with his wife, Sumi, and their two adorable children, Amit and Neta.

WATCH DAN ARIELY'S TED TALKS

Dan Ariely's TED Talks, available for free at TED.com, are the companion to *Payoff*.

PHOTO: BRET HARTMAN/TED

Barry Schwartz
The way we think about work is broken
What makes work satisfying? Apart
from a paycheck, there are intangible
values that, Barry Schwartz suggests,
our current way of thinking about
work simply ignores. It's time to
stop thinking of workers as cogs on a
wheel.

David Brooks
The social animal
Columnist David Brooks unpacks
new insights into human nature from
the cognitive sciences—insights
with massive implications for
economics and politics as well as our
own self-knowledge. In a talk full of
humor, he shows how you can't hope
to understand humans as separate
individuals making choices based on
their conscious awareness.

Dan Pink
The puzzle of motivation
Career analyst Dan Pink examines
the puzzle of motivation, starting
with a fact that social scientists know
but most managers don't: Traditional
rewards aren't always as effective
as we think. Listen for illuminating
stories—and maybe, a way forward.

Dan Gilbert
The surprising science of happiness
Dan Gilbert, author of *Stumbling on
Happiness*, challenges the idea that
we'll be miserable if we don't get what
we want. Our "psychological immune
system" lets us feel truly happy even
when things don't go as planned.

When Strangers Meet
by Kio Stark

When Strangers Meet reveals the transformative possibility of talking to people you don't know—how these beautiful interruptions in daily life can change you and the world we share. Kio Stark argues for the surprising pleasures of talking to strangers.

Asteroid Hunters
by Carrie Nugent

Everyone's got questions about asteroids. What are they and where do they come from? And most urgently: Are they going to hit the earth? Asteroid hunter Carrie Nugent reveals everything we know about asteroids, and how new technology may help us prevent a natural disaster.

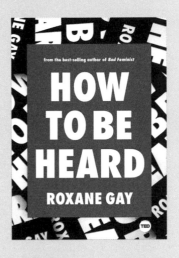

How to Be Heard
by Roxane Gay

Full of practical wisdom that anyone pursuing a creative life will find fascinating and useful, this book explores the complex concept of being heard. Investigated with her signature bravery, wit, and honesty Roxane Gay reveals how to use your voice so people will listen.

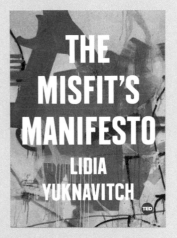

The Misfit's Manifesto
by Lidia Yuknavitch

Misfit: A person who missed fitting in, a person who fits in badly, a person who is poorly adapted to new situations and environments. It's a shameful word, a word no one typically tries to own. Until now. Bestselling author Lidia Yuknavitch reveals why she is proud to be a misfit.

ABOUT TED BOOKS

TED Books are small books about big ideas. They're short enough to read in a single sitting, but long enough to delve deep into a topic. The wide-ranging series covers everything from architecture to business, space travel to love, and is perfect for anyone with a curious mind and an expansive love of learning.

Each TED Book is paired with a related TED Talk, available online at TED.com. The books pick up where the talks leave off An 18-minute speech can plant a seed or spark the imagination, but many talks create a need to go deeper, to learn more, to tell a longer story. TED Books fill this need.

TED is a nonprofit devoted to spreading ideas, usually in the form of short, powerful talks (eighteen minutes or less) but also through books, animation, radio programs, and events. TED began in 1984 as a conference where Technology, Entertainment, and Design converged, and today covers almost every topic—from science to business to global issues—in more than 100 languages. Meanwhile, independently run TEDx events help share ideas in communities around the world.

TED is a global community, welcoming people from every discipline and culture who seek a deeper understanding of the world. We believe passionately in the power of ideas to change attitudes, lives, and, ultimately, our future. On TED.com, we're building a clearinghouse of free knowledge from the world's most inspired thinkers—and a community of curious souls to engage with ideas and each other, both online and at TED and TEDx events around the world, all year long.

In fact, everything we do—from the TED Radio Hour to the projects sparked by the TED Prize, from the global TEDx community to the TED-Ed lesson series—is driven by this goal: How can we best spread great ideas?

TED is owned by a nonprofit, nonpartisan foundation.